# From Platb
# Kilimanj

via Mount Stanley, Mou  ....nya
and Mont-aux-Sources...

Self-published

Walk in Wild Places

https://walkinwildplaces.com/

Harry Loots

harry.loots@walkinwildplaces.com

First published 2020 by Walk in Wild Places
https://walkinwildplaces.com/

A catalogue record for this book is available from the British Library

ISBN (printed): 978-1-8382999-0-3

This book is also available in Kindle format
ISBN: 978-1-8382999-1-0

# TABLE OF CONTENTS

# Dedication

To the guides, porters, muleteers, and cooks who made this possible. To André, who climbed Africa's three highest mountains with me, and Mandy who joined us for part of the way. I could have done this without you but, it would not have been half as much fun.

To my children, who tolerated my absences. At least one of whom constantly worried that I was going to be abducted by terrorists in a remote African village. To my girlfriend who lit a candle in a church in Sicily on the day André and I were descending Kilimanjaro.

To my family and friends who supported me throughout this journey. Without your love and support this would have been just another trip to a mountain. Knowing how much love and care there was out there made a memorable adventure an unforgettable one. And, finally, to the long list of friends who have spent many days and hours climbing mountains with me. Making memories and forming lifelong friendships. You know who you are.

PS! I tried to remember as many names as possible in the 'Climbing mates' chapter, but I'm sure I will have left out a few. Please remind me so that I can add your name.

# FOREWORD

I was six or seven years old when a visiting school nurse told me: "Ai my kind, jou ou voetjies is so lekker plat. Jy moet nooit te ver wil gaan stap nie!" which roughly translates to "My child, your little feet are very flat. You should never try to walk too far!".

I ignored the advice.

Fifty-three years, thousands of kilometres, and many mountain tops later, I stood on top of Kilimanjaro, the highest mountain in Africa. Flat feet and all!

This is how I got there.

I didn't grow up in a mountaineering family, but it may have been a family outing that triggered what was to become a life-long passion. I was four or five years old when my parents walked to the top of Platberg, the flat-topped mountain that towers above Harrismith. I remember that I was unhappy at being left behind. Whether this was just me being annoyed at parents leaving me at home with my Granny, while they went out and had fun, or envy that they got to walk to the top of the mountain and I did not, I can't remember. Apparently, for weeks afterwards I asked questions about the trip and what they saw on the mountain. It was also the only time I know of that my parents climbed a mountain.

Perhaps it was this that planted the seed… Or perhaps it was after my first trip to the top of the Drakensberg. I was six or seven years old by then. It was a Sunday school outing, and the group leader was Oom Dawie, I seem to recall.

In my brown leather satchel, I normally used for my schoolbooks, I was carrying a flask of water and the sandwiches my mother made for me. An orange or two. My jersey was tied around my waist and my plastic raincoat was stuffed into the satchel. I was probably wearing shorts and a flannel shirt. On my 'flat' feet I had my good leather shoes with rubber soles that I normally wore to church on Sundays.

The trip was to the Drakensberg area us locals referred to as Mont-aux-Sources. But in fact we went no further than the old Mountain Club hut, a few kilometres from the peak. At the time, and for years after, I thought Mont-aux-Sources was the highest point in the Drakensberg. A trip to Mont-aux-Sources carried with it bragging rights. Plus there was the added excitement that you would see where water bubbled out of the earth. The 'sources', to start the Tugela and Elands Rivers, and a tributary to the Orange River! One of these rivers ends up in the Indian Ocean and the other two in the Atlantic – more than 1400km apart.

To get to 'Mont-aux-Sources' one walks steeply upwards via a series of zigzags to a path below the North Face of the Sentinel. And then along a slightly rising contour path to end beneath a solid rock wall equipped with a chain ladder.

What I remember from this first trip was how the world below got smaller and smaller as I zigged and zagged upwards. And the feeling of disconnection as I walked along the contour path. The valleys below appearing to float beneath my feet, as I made distance and gained altitude. Then, as we turned a corner, in front of us was a huge gap between two solid rock walls. On the left, when you looked up, was the chain ladder. Two strands of cold, and rusty-looking chain snaking down the smoke grey rock wall, with metal rungs that seemed to go up and up and up into the blue sky above. Then, almost too soon, it was my turn to climb...

What I remember even more vividly than the walk was my very first experience of climbing the chain ladder. Gripping the rungs tight with both hands. Putting my rubber soled shoes on the rungs, one at a time. Moving one hand up; gripping tightly. Then moving the other hand up to a higher rung, gripping tightly. Then a foot moving up, and then another; then again hands, moving up one at a time, and repeat.

I remember being worried that the weight of the satchel on my back would make me fall backwards. This worry increasing at probably about the same rate as the drop below me increased. I also remember worrying that my hands or shoes might slip off the cold damp metal bars. And there were probably another hundred worries running through my head. One for each time I took a giant step up to the next rung. Making sure I didn't lean too far back and overbalance, I gradually made my way to the top.

Harry Loots

And then I stood on top of the Drakensberg! For the first time! In complete awe of the dramatic drops and the roughly sculptured rock faces that guarded her. In my mind, I had reached the very top of the world. Every fear that had gripped my six-year-old body evaporated and was replaced by a sense of 'Wow! I made it.' Later, peering over the edge of the escarpment at the Tugela falls, and having lunch near the Mountain Club hut, all added to the sense of adventure. And perhaps on that day I knew that I wanted to stand on top of many mountains.

I also remember how disappointed I was when Oom Dawie decided that it would be too dangerous for us six-year-olds to descend via the chain ladder. We had to return via a boring rock-strewn gully that led back to the contour path.

I there-and-then resolved that I would go back to the Drakensberg and go up and down the chain ladder on my own. I did! Many times over in the coming years and continue to do so whenever I get the opportunity. Sometimes, I'd scramble up the Standard route on the Sentinel. The imposing buttress which stands tall above the path to the chain ladder. With its mind-blowing views across the Amphitheatre, the Devil's Tooth, and miles and miles and miles beyond.

So, perhaps it was this first trip to the top of the Drakensberg that set me on this path of climbing mountains. Discovering new summits and intricately carved rock-faces with interlocking structures creating unique shapes. Seeing plants and the trees as I wend my way, dazzling me with their colours. Wondering at the shape of their leaves and how they manage to survive in the most unbelievable and sometimes inhospitable places. Amazed at birds that cross the skies in effortless flight: gliding, tumbling, diving, hovering. Birds who make untraceable paths in the air. Playfully following and watching me as I make my way along a mountain path. Sometimes venturing closer as I eat my lunch at a resting spot. The sounds that surround me. The whistling of the wind through sky-tall trees, around rock fortresses and up never-ending rock-flutes. The swish-swish-swish as swallows and swifts dive headlong past me to the depths below. Rustling leaves and grasses waving in the moving air. Thunder rolling down a ridge while blinding flashes pierce the darkened skies. Water rushing headlong over stones...

Or perhaps I started climbing mountains because, as Mallory said, it's there.

Growing up at the foot of a mountain meant that I was able to learn outdoor skills in a relatively safe environment. Our house was situated at the edge of town. With a clear view and easy access to both the fields and the nearby stream, known as K-spruit in polite conversation, or more commonly as 'Kakspruit'. As children we spent many hours convincing ourselves that we were the new incarnations of Robin Hood and his Merry men. Or whoever the heroes were in the latest adventure story we were reading. Just beyond this field and stream was the start of our mountain.

Platberg – our mountain

Platberg towers majestically above the little Free State town of Harrismith. It is home of the famous Harrismith Bergresies[1]. In 1947, it may even have been internationally famous for a little while! This was when a young Princess Elizabeth visited our mountain during a Royal tour of South Africa.

Rising from one-thousand-six-hundred metres above sea level to nearly two-thousand-four-hundred metres, Platberg really is a flat mountain. The nine-kilometre-long plateau with a width of more than one-and-a-half kilometres in some places, averages between two-thousand-two-hundred and two-thousand-three-hundred metres in height. The highest point, 2394m, only about hundred-and-fifty metres higher than the lowest point.

This is where I spent many of my days during weekends and school holidays. While other boys were learning how to play rugby, I was learning how to play in the mountains. To survive in the wilderness and, more importantly, developing a love for the freedom of the outdoors.

I was never good at rugby, and not particularly interested in playing, so I never made it beyond the third team. Which meant that I only played a few times a year, and also meant that I had time on weekends to wander around the slopes of Platberg.

Part of this learning came from being in the local Voortrekker troop. Voortrekkers were a South African equivalent to the Boy Scout movement. Ironically enough, part of the inspiration for the Boy Scout movement originated in South Africa. Robert Baden-Powell was stationed in Mafeking during the second Anglo-Boer war. Besieged for months, he started using the local Cadet Corps to run messages, help

---

[1] Mountain race

the wounded and act as lookouts. The cadets impressed Baden-Powell with the way they took to their tasks. A few years later he discovered that boys were using his military manual, 'Aids to Scouting', as a guide to outdoor fun. This spurred Baden-Powell on to form the Boy Scouts, which had their first camp in 1907.

After the Anglo-Boer war, there was a very strong anti-British sentiment among Afrikaners in South Africa. Understandable given the thousands of women and children that died in the British Concentration camps. This gave rise to Afrikaner nationalism ideology. One of its aims having been to keep English and Afrikaner youth on separate social paths. Thus, in 1913 the Voortrekker movement was founded. Aimed at Afrikaans-speaking youth, with its values firmly rooted in Afrikaner nationalism. The Boy Scouts soon diversified and became an international movement. The Voortrekkers remained exactly as it started: a movement for Afrikaans speaking youth.

I joined the Voortrekkers either because my mom or dad said I should, or because some of my friends joined, and I joined them. I don't know. What I do know is that from a young age I was learning how to tie knots, cook in the outdoors, set up a camp in a way that would both protect me from the wind and rain and cause the least amount of impact to the area.

Blissfully unaware that the Voortrekker movement was rooted in Afrikaner nationalism, I loved the camaraderie and opportunities for adventure that it brought. And it provided me with an environment where I could learn outdoor skills which I may not have been able to do otherwise. (We had to wait until I was about sixteen years old for the Boy Scout movement to find its way to Harrismith.)

One of my earliest camping and trekking trips happened in my first or second school year. Our troop leader was Chris van Zyl who was in his final school years. We pitched our canvas tent in the little oakwood copse above Harrismith. I don't remember what we learnt on that trip. But I remember some of Chris's schoolmates, possibly Arrie Schreiber and Guillaume Reitz, coming up in the evening and scaring the wits out of us.

Platberg – at sunset; from the botanical gardens area

My main climbing partner was Freddy Gray. Freddy died in a car accident when we were twenty years old, so we never climbed the big mountains we both dreamt of together. Our frequent companion was Gerard Hansen, who is also no longer with us. Gerard lived on the edge of town, near the Municipal Waterworks, where many of the paths that lead up the mountainside begin. Starting from Gerard's house on a Saturday morning, we would walk up one of the many paths that made their way past the Municipal Waterworks and through the pine forest. Up into the gullies that give the mountain its distinctive look.

Harry Loots

Occasionally we were joined by JP de Witt, André Landman, and other friends. We'd spend many glorious hours exploring nooks and crannies, soaking up the sun and watching the birds and dassies[2]. Some days we'd come across antelope going about their daily routine.

Some days Freddy and I would go up One-Man's Pass and down Zig Zag Pass, following the route of the mountain race. Some nights we'd spend in the oakwood copse above town. Then as we got older, we went higher up to the prominent overhang halfway up One-Man's Pass, with a thick woollen blanket for a sleeping bag. Our dinners were simple. The kind that a ten-year-old can prepare without their mother's help. A can of baked beans and bully beef warmed up over an open fire and fresh bread from the baker. (Probably not the cuisine that the future Queen Elizabeth would have been treated to on her visit to our mountain.) Preparing 'dinner' often resulted in me coming home with blisters on my fingers – from taking hot cans out of open fires. Water came from mountain streams or drips off the mountainside during dry seasons.

On some weekends, Freddy and I climbed on the basalt rock flutes that guarded the summit. Sometimes we'd belay each other with washing line cord. Many years later when I climbed here with Mountain Club members, I realised how many mistakes we made. Not only with our choice of climbing rope, but also our technique, which, if either of us had fallen, would have resulted in a serious accident. Alongside this realization there was also pride. Knowing that we had climbed some of these rock faces long before they were being claimed as new routes. With a washing line!

---

[2] Rock hyrax

As our confidence grew, so did our curiosity. Still ignoring the school nurse's advice, I started wandering further afield. Some weekends we'd follow the river as far as Swinburne. Other times we'd find ourselves on one of the many sandstone outcrops dotted around Harrismith.

Then, as teenagers, we started looking towards the distant peaks of the Drakensberg.

The Drakensberg - Sentinel peak on the right of the amphitheatre.
Picture taken from Royal Natal National Park

## MONT-AUX-SOURCES

For years, I believed that the highest point in the Drakensberg was Mont-aux-Sources. So, I grew up thinking that if I get to the top of Mont-aux-Sources I will have climbed to the highest point in the Drakensberg, or 'berg' as it's colloquially known.

To get to Mont-aux-Sources you had to climb to the top of the escarpment using the chain ladder. This meant either starting your hike in Royal Natal National Park or find your way to the Sentinel car park.

Mike managed to get into the cowl of our tent. André had to spend a cold and miserable night outside, inside my plastic survival bag and the few extra clothes we could spare.

He survived both the cold and the survival bag. He also survived a few other incidents, including one where he had to be resuscitated twice. André and I climbed together regularly after this, until I moved to Cape Town in the mid-eighties. After this I'd see him and other Natal mates mainly during the summer holidays. Then I moved to England in the mid-nineties and didn't see my friend again until 2008.

The occasion was the twenty-fifth anniversary of the Amajuba Section of the MCSA. The club that I had started in 1983 with the help of other MCSA members. Wiv and Joan von Willich, Dougal Drummond, Frank du Toit, Doug Lyon, Christine Glasspool, Tjaart van der Walt, Giel Prins, and a few others. Some of my most memorable mountaineering trips were had with the club…

Like the time we left the Isandlwana Police Station after eleven in the morning (some claim it was even later). Apparently, I had been at a party the night before so took my time getting to the base. We duly left with packs, packed for a three-day stay on the escarpment.

I aimed to reach the escarpment via the Rockeries Pass that evening. The best part of twenty kilometres of walking and about sixteen-hundred metres height gain.

At the foot of the pass Frikkie van Zyl decided to put up camp. Angus Drummond, Richard Groenewegen, Thea Groenewegen, Gary Gifford, and I carried on. We arrived at the top of the pass in the dark and in the rain. And discovered that half the second tent we were supposed to have with us was at the foot of the pass with Frikkie. We pitched our tent. Squeezed in. All five of us. In a two-man tent. Did synchronised turns all night long. Thea and Richard sleeping next to each other[4]. We climbed one of the Mnweni Needles the next day.

On another occasion we woke at the foot of the Mnweni pass after hiking for three days across the escarpment. It was my fortieth birthday and Jane Hill and Henriette Gibson produced cake, candles, and champagne to celebrate.

Not forgetting the Christmas parties we had in Xeni Cave. Black tie affairs with five-course dinners with some of the best people I've known. Herman Behrens, Rob Campbell, Beryl Gronland, Jane Hill, Henriette, Colin, Julie-Anne and William Gibson, Thea Groenewegen, Dougal, Lynn, Angus, Ian and Rowan Drummond, Gill Tresise, Jan van der Velden, and others.

Nor trips to the top of the Drakensberg with Doug Lyon, Chris Steenkamp, and Frank du Toit. And someone knocking the pot of rice over...

Sadly, not all of these people made it to the twenty-fifth anniversary dinner. But André did. This started a sequence of events which would lead us to the top of Kilimanjaro a few years later.

In 2009, a year after the twenty-fifth anniversary celebrations, André joined me and members of the MCSA Amajuba section on a hiking and climbing trip to the Dolomites, the mountain range in Northern Italy that had become my 'mountain home' since moving to the UK. A couple of years later André was back in the Dolomites. And this time we were joined by Adrian Jardin (Pigmy).

---

[4] They got married a few years later.

I had been on Mount Kenya in 2008. An unseasonal snowfall the night before I was due to start the climb to the summit of Batian (5188m), made me call off the climb. With further bad weather rolling in, I retreated. Moses and I reached the top of Point Lenana (4985m) – aka the 'tourist summit', the day before. I also had a headache from hell that afternoon. Altitude sickness. My own fault. I went up Point Lenana far too quickly and paid the price. The cook gave me lots of lemon tea. By early evening I was feeling almost human again. Perhaps the lemon tea he prescribed was the cure... Point Lenana is small consolation for climbers. The real prize is the twin summits of Batian and Nelion – and I had every intention of going back to finish what I started in 2008.

Heading to Shipton Camp with Moses; Mount Kenya in the background

At some point in July 2010, André and I started talking about climbing Mount Kenya. We talked about going in March of the next year. Then came massive political unrest and disruption during one of the most tumultuous election periods in Kenyan history. We stopped planning before we got started and waited for the dust to settle.

The next time we 'planned' on going, work got in the way. Then family events got in the way. So, we just kept talking, year after year. At some stage we also talked about climbing both Mount Stanley and Mount Kenya – the one to warm up and acclimatise for the other.

Strangely, neither of us talked about or were particularly interested in climbing Kilimanjaro. Both of us thought about it as a tourist trap, so best avoided. I often joked that I would join the shuffle to the top one day when I got issued with my Zimmer frame…

### THEN WE THOUGHT OF CLIMBING KILIMANJARO…

And then, in 2015, while we were playing in the Dolomites, we decided that if we were going to do Mount Kenya, or Mount Stanley and Mount Kenya, we might as well do Mount Kilimanjaro as well. All three summits of the highest African mountains in one adventure. Mount Stanley, the highest peak on the Rwenzori mountains from the Uganda side. Batian on Mount Kenya via the Normal route (a technical climb), and Uhuru Peak on Kilimanjaro. Most people would have considered climbing any one of the three to be enough of a challenge. Just the height we would gain vertically – nearly ten kilometres – would have been enough of a challenge for some people. That height, by the way, is more than one and a half times the total height that climbers on Everest cover. Challenging? Yes. But what an adventure. From the moment I started planning it to the moment I stood on top of Kilimanjaro with André, this was a grand adventure.

Never had any of those... but I did have a strong vision, even as a teenager that one day I would climb to the top of Kilimanjaro.

Freddy Gray and I hatched a plan when we were about sixteen or seventeen years old. South African passport holders were not welcome in Tanzania. Thanks to the then government's apartheid policies. But we could get into Kenya. So we planned to travel to Kenya, then sneak across the border and make our way up Kilimanjaro from the Kenya side.

Our plans were thwarted not by lack of ambition, but due to lack of funds. Perhaps fortunately. Later on, with tourist numbers increasing on Kilimanjaro, I felt that Kilimanjaro had become a tourist trap and that there were other mountains to climb. So even this item got scratched off my non-existent bucket list...

To get fit I flew to Tenerife to climb the 3,718m high Teide. Then to Morocco where I walked in the Rif Mountains. Next, I moved onto the Atlas Mountains where I summited Northern Africa's highest peak, Jbel Toubkal (4167m). Then came a trip to Ethiopia to climb Ras Dejen (4533m) in the Simien mountains in Ethiopia. It was here that I first met Mandy, who, when I told her about our planned adventure, asked to join us on our climb of Mount Kenya. I still don't know a lot more about Mandy than that she is an American from Wisconsin who lived in Hawaii and who was in Africa with a plan to work her way from South to North Africa. But what I do know about her is that she is gutsy, resilient and a great hiking companion. Her original African travel plan went awry, and she ended up in Egypt, from where she was now making her way back South. (Tip: never plan your African travel. Just arrive and see where the wind blows you.)

A few months later I met André in Nairobi airport, en route to Entebbe airport in Uganda. It was 27 July 2016, and we were finally embarking on our grand adventure.

But before André and I met up in Nairobi, on the way to the top of Kilimanjaro, I stood on top of several other African summits - each with their own charm and their own story…

So, there I was, soaking up the pale sun on a nudist beach below the colourful Montaña Roja with its rust and sulphur coloured strewn rock. Stumbled upon. Like most other things during the week I was there.

It was my last day in Tenerife. I had failed to achieve my objective of climbing the 3,718 metres high volcano Teide. But I was perfectly happy having spent the week hiking along various interesting and charming paths.

When you mention Tenerife, many people immediately think of Playa de las Américas. The purpose-built holiday resort on the southwestern coastline of Tenerife. Man-made beaches with white sand imported from Africa. Man-made entertainment with its hotels, bars, casinos, strip clubs. Probably not the first place one might think of visiting if you want to go hiking.

If you look closer at the map though, you'll see that the largest of the Canary Islands is basically a volcanic mountain. With the highest point Teide, right in the middle of it. This 3,718-metre-high volcano, which last erupted in 1909 was my target when I set off in April. Three months before we made our way to East Africa. To acclimatise, and then move onto the over 4000-ers.

Alas, it was not to be. I had booked to spend the night in the Refugio de Altavista, the mountain hut situated at 3270m. About halfway up the eastern slopes, it allows you to ascend the peak without the red tape involved of obtaining a separate permit. As long as you're off the summit path before 09.00. From the summit of Pico Teide, I planned to descend west. Past the mini crater of Pico Veije (3104m), until I reached the national road. From where I was hoping to hop on a bus, or hitch-hike to the nearest town and find accommodation. It was the only part of the trip I had pre-planned. I was informed the afternoon before that all paths had been closed due to a snowfall on the mountain. I contacted the park authorities. Tried to persuade them that I had crampons, ice axe, climbing experience on glaciers and peaks higher than Mount Teide. Even pleaded with them. To no avail. The path is closed. A bureaucratic red line had been drawn. Teide was out of bounds. You can look at it. But you can't touch it.

So, I had to find alternatives from the guidebook I had brought with me. In the end I stumbled onto some of the nicest coastal hikes I've come across. Nothing desperate. But not to be taken lightly either.

For the first day's walking I picked a route across the 435m-high Montaña de Guaza, then along the coast, stopping off to swim at regular intervals, past the disused lighthouse at Faro de Rasca and on to Las Galletas, where I got a bus back to Los Cristianos. The plants, and rock formations along the coast, the informal settlements, banana plantations, all made for a fascinating day's walk. And the ice cream at Las Galletas well deserved.

The next pick from the pages of the guidebook I had brought along, was the interesting looking hike to the Masca gorge. The hike turning out to be a super pleasant descent of a gorge starting 600m above sea level and ending with a swim below the imposing cliffs of Los Gigantes before boarding a boat and heading back towards Puerto de Los Gigantes.

I abandoned the next day's walk. After I got desperately lost trying to get to a ledge system which would have allowed me to do a high-level traverse above the cliff of Los Gigantes. The start of this route was through numerous disused mining tunnels. And there were moments while I was in the belly of the earth, with just a headlamp to light my way that I felt very alone. A rusty abandoned cocopan, in a valley with a precarious drop, made me realise that I had taken a wrong branch of the valley. I agreed with the sensible part of me to turn back. A couple of hours later, having managed to find my way back through the tunnels, I was sitting at a little roadside café, drinking an ice-cold beer shandy, whilst I waited for the next bus back to the hotel. Beaten but not defeated.

Along the way I met and chatted to young people, families, and pensioners who spent half the year living in this little paradise. On another day I was invited to have a massage in a makeshift tent in an informal settlement. At another informal settlement I was offered some tobacco with a kick. I also came across a fascinating array of plant life which added a welcome shade of green to the red-brown desert-like terrain. All making for some interesting walking, with my final walk leading to the discovery of the nudist beach in a protected cove at the base of Montaña Roja.

A beach walk to Montaña Roja – the peak on the left

The great irony did not escape me. Each unplanned event just happened – bringing with it a trove of unexpected discoveries. Whilst the one part of the trip I had actually planned, was the one part that never took place…

## NAKED IN MOROCCO

I'm lying naked on a cement slab in Tangiers, barely an hour after I arrived from Chefchaouen, where I had been hiking for the past few days. And no, in case you're wondering, I'm not dead. I'm in a hammam, getting scrubbed clean after a long warm dusty drive from Chefchaouen. A much-needed wash before I boarded the overnight train to Marrakech.

The matronly figure who scrubbed me is pouring fresh clean water over my body. It creates a not unpleasant stinging sensation. I'm still in a state of surprise! This motherly figure who had scrubbed my back and legs, had also washed places that only my mother would have been allowed to wash. And then only when I was very small…

What started as shock turned into philosophical resignation. I came to accept that this kindly woman scrubs people. It's her job, and when I did, I relaxed and the scrubbing of 'private places' simply became a part of the routine…

Tangiers is one of my favourite Moroccan cities. An evening in Tangiers has a sense of old-world charm and romance about it. There's a sense of nostalgia, when you can sit on a balcony and sip a cocktail while local people are going about their daily business below you. In much the same way as they have been for centuries. The setting always makes me think of the film *Casablanca*. Palms swaying in a light sea breeze. Elegant waiters in ageing establishments with thick carpets. Fans whirring away above. Music drifting across from the overhead speakers. Mixing with the sound of traffic and people below.

So, before I headed to the train station, I found myself a restaurant with a balcony overlooking the local plain. Slowly sipping my mojito while waiting for my dinner to be served. My thoughts crossing back to the past few days' hiking in the Rif Mountains near Chefchaouen. Yes, I could have gone hiking in the foothills of the Atlas. But I find the scenery in the foothills of the Atlas quite repetitive, whereas the Rif mountains offer a more varied environment. Waterfalls, forests, valleys, mountain tops.

I had hired a local guide, Mohamed. Not because I couldn't find my way, but because I knew I would be crossing land where cannabis is grown. And that some growers have been aggressive in the past towards strangers. Mohamed, a qualified teacher, turns out to be great company. His biggest gripe being that unless he greased palms, he wouldn't get a teaching post at a local school. Refusing to grease palms, he spends his time guiding people in the mountains around Chefchaouen.

Our first trip is to Jebel El-Kelaa (1616m), the peak above Chefchaouen. We took a direct route up the valley, rather than the long-winded path shown on the tourist map, passing a rubbish dump, which spoils the walk somewhat. But you soon leave that behind and start climbing.

A few hundred metres above Chefchaouen I spotted tiny little green shoots with a very distinctive leaf pattern. Cannabis. Mohamed spots them at the same time. We were in the midst of a cannabis plantation. One of many.

It started to rain. A little higher up a local appeared and started talking to Mohamed in quite animated fashion and obviously not happy that we were there. Mohamed explained that we were passing through, on our way to the summit.

I greet the man with a friendly "Salaam a leikum" to which he responded in the pattern. This seemed to soften his attitude. I asked Mohamed to ask him if this was his farm, and if he lived here. Showing interest in what he was doing, breaks the ice. He pointed towards a rock and corrugated iron shelter and invited us to join him. Out of the rain.

Inside the shelter is a little boy. Seven, eight years old. His oldest son. There's a small fire going, providing warmth for him and the boy. Next to it is a tinpot for boiling water and making tea. Mint tea, which he sets about doing almost straight away.

Once he stopped seeing us as a threat, this man turned out to be a thoroughly friendly and welcoming host. I ask him questions about his work. He explains the difference between marijuana and hash to me via Mohamed. Then we talk about his boy and the boy's education. What is he learning on the farm? What subjects is he doing at school? We have more tea. Staying dry and out of the rain. We've abandoned the idea of going to the summit and getting cold and wet. After a few hours, Mohamed and I said goodbye to our host, and made our way back down the steep hill back to Chefchaouen. Almost reluctantly…

There's a bigger picture here, easy to overlook if you simply think to yourself – this man is a cannabis farmer. He's growing a drug. An illegal substance. From a distance you see a provider of illegal drugs. Then you talk to the man and meet a human being. Is he happy to be a cannabis farmer, I want to know? No. 'It's dangerous work', he says. 'Why not do another job?', I asked. 'What other job?', he responds with a shrug. 'There's not enough work.'

You come to understand how hard he has to work to produce a single bag of cannabis so that he can earn enough to feed his family. And to feed them for a whole year he has to produce several bags a year. His work does not stop at growing the product either. Once he's grown and dried the plants, he has to deliver it to smugglers. They cross the Mediterranean Sea at night in fast motorboats, delivering the goods to the European shores[5]. From here it is sold on to local dealers. He doesn't like dealing with the smugglers. Thinks they are dangerous. But he's dependent on them for buying his product.

By the end of our chat, I have seen a completely different side of the story and have developed an empathy for this gently spoken man. I ask myself if there is much difference between this cannabis farmer and the tobacco growers in America, or the wine growers in the South of France...

I will try to visit this man again when I get back to the Rif mountains. Even if it's just to give him the pictures I took of him and his boy. To remind him of the day they extended their hospitality to a total stranger.

The next day Mohamed and I hike to the magnificent waterfall at Akchour. It was beautiful and green and interesting. It was everything I had expected this relatively unknown area to be. But it was nowhere near as interesting as sitting and chatting and having tea with a cannabis farmer.

I spent my final morning in Chefchaouen walking through the streets of the blue city. Stopping for a cup of tea at a café overlooking the town square below the imposing ancient castle. At the medina I buy a djellaba – the dress-like garment with a large hood made of wool. Worn by local men, it will keep you warm even in the coldest mountain winds. After lunch with Mohamed it was time to head back to Tangiers.

A hot afternoon strapped to the front seat of an ancient Mercedes, whose air-conditioning dated back to pre-Noah architecture and which blew out more hot and dusty air than what was coming through the windows, prompted me to visit the local hammam for a wash...

---

[5] Moroccan growers supply an estimated thirty-five percent of Europe's cannabis needs.

Later that evening I boarded the overnight train that would take me to Marrakech. Spending the night on the top coach while an amorous young heterosexual couple were occupying the lower coach in a male only compartment. Illegally. But no-one was checking. They were considerate enough to turn the lights out when I asked them. They even turned the music off. But I'm not sure that was an improvement. Other sounds now filled the darkened cabin…

Hassan's brother met me on arrival in Marrakech and directed me to the taxi that would drive me to Imlil. I was on my way to the Atlas Mountains, where Hassan and I were going to do a fast ascent of Jbel Toubkal. The 4167-metre-high peak is a perfect opportunity for me to get fitter and better acclimatised.

I've climbed Jbel Toubkal twice. The first time was with Hassan and my Scottish friend Andy Borthwick just before Christmas in 2010. Snow covered the mountain to below 1600 metres. We spent a freezing night in the refuge at 3200 metres. Had an icy cold start to the climb the next morning. I remember my hands being so cold that at one stage Hassan had to help me close my bag after I drank some water. The amazing view from the top made up for every bit of suffering. Standing on the snow-covered summit of the highest mountain in North Africa and looking down on the endless scorched Sahara Desert below is an amazing, even if somewhat incongruous experience.

The second trip was with the Newcastle gang. Richard and Thea Groenewegen, Zelda Willemse and Moira Burger. It was in May 2013. The peak was covered in snow from a short way above the hut to the summit. Which I was grateful for as it makes for a much easier ascent than battling up the bare scree slope you would otherwise encounter.

On the day we made our way to the summit, there was a wind blowing. I got to the top about half an hour before the rest and was nearly frozen by the time they got there. But the views and the hugs of my friends made up for it.

This time however it was to be a lightning-fast ascent. A 'get-fit-and-acclimatised' exercise. Straight off the train in Marrakech, into a taxi. Drive to Imlil. Trek to the refuge at 3200 metres. Climb to the summit at 4167 metres the next morning. Descend all the way back to Imlil. Drive back to Marrakech. With lunch at Hassan's house on the way back thrown in.

Trekking to Jbel Toubkal

A muleteer heading for the hut took on my sleeping bag and spare clothes, washing kit, etc., as part load. Hassan and I carried light. We stayed at the Refuge Toubkal Les Mouflons, which I've come to prefer thanks mainly to the much better heating in the common area. I also like the people who run the refuge. Guides seem to prefer the other refuge, Refuge du Toubkal – a French Alpine Club refuge. Not sure why. Climbing in a freezing wind, Hassan and I made it to the top with a few other diehards. Several other parties having decided that the wind is too much to continue and turning back. That's besides the few that developed all kinds of symptoms which prevented them from starting that morning. Getting to the summit is not just a physical exercise. It's easy to give in to mental fatigue and give up before you get to the top. I know. I've been there.

And before you wonder, 'now where did he get naked this time?'... this time it wasn't me.

Ras Dejen, traditionally spelled Ras Dashen in English, is Africa's fifth highest mountain (and 14th highest peak). At 4,550 metres it was a lot closer to the 5000 plus metres we were going to face when we got to Mount Stanley. It would also put me a step closer to being acclimatised at higher altitudes.

But that wasn't the only reason I wanted to climb Ras Dejen. The Simien mountains have interested me for a long time. From the pictures I had seen, I was intrigued by the appearance of this majestic mountain. Close to the Horn of Africa, and looking very similar to the mountains where I grew up – the Drakensberg (albeit a 1000m higher).

I was also fascinated by the country itself. I wanted to meet our great-great-great grandmother Lucy, and I wanted to find out more about the country that gave the world Haile Selassie. Ethiopia's last emperor. Yah to many Rastafarians. One of Africa's most powerful leaders of the 20th century. Selassie's pro-western views led to Ethiopia becoming a charter member of the United Nations in 1923. He later presided over the formation and served as the first chairman of the Organization of African Unity (later the African Union).

In November 1930, Ras Tafari was crowned Emperor of Ethiopia, taking on the name Haile Selassie (meaning 'Power of the Trinity').

The Rastafari movement who reveres Selassie as incarnation of God (Yah), derived their name from 'Ras' + 'Tafari'. The Ethiopian noble title 'Ras' meaning prince combined with his birth name (Tafari).

Widely regarded as having laid the foundation for modern day Ethiopia, he was a strong believer in the power of education as a catalyst for modernization.

In National Museum of Ethiopia in Addis Ababa I finally met Lucy. When discovered in the Awash Valley in Ethiopia in 1974, Lucy was the oldest known and most complete skeleton of a female of the hominin species *Australopithecus afarensis*. Lucy predates our own species *Homo Sapiens* by about two million years. The skeleton, dated at more than three million years old, was reconstructed and discovered to be 1.1m tall, and estimated to have weighed about 29kg. Lucy, like myself, had flat feet. Her pelvis and leg bones were almost identical to modern humans. This indicated that Lucy and other members of her species stood and walked upright.

In the same museum I was able to view Haile Selassie and his wife's separate bathrooms. I also saw his uniforms. I learnt about the history of the Ethiopian people. Viewed many examples of artwork dating back hundreds of years. Looked at reconstructions of shelters showing how they lived in ancient times. I learnt about their religious affinities and visited the modern university. Late afternoon I had a drive-through tour of the marketplace – the biggest open-air market in Africa.

The next day I visited a museum in honour of the hundreds of thousands that were killed during the dictatorial communist rule that started in 1974 when Haile Selassie was deposed. It left me deep in thought about the cruelty of our fellow human beings. And it continues even today in every part of the world. I also shopped for a few simple essentials, like snack bars, and drew enough cash to be able to pay the support team I was going to hire for my trek.

In the evening, I discovered an Ethiopian folk music and dance venue. Where music was made with a mixture of traditional and modern instruments. Groups of people performed song and dance routines depicting people at work, hunting, at war, falling in love, and just about any human activity you can think of.

I also ate something which had me dying for the next twenty-four hours. Due to fly to Gondar early the next morning, from where I was to travel to the Simien mountains, I was seriously considering cancelling flights and calling the undertakers.

I somehow managed to drag myself to the airport. Drank lots of flat sugary drinks and water to keep hydrated. Boarded the flight and prayed that the toilets worked. Landed in Gondar; took a taxi to the hotel and then deposited myself in my hotel room for the rest of the day while I was slowly dying! Dinner was the first time I managed to have anything to eat. Bread and pasta. I even managed to keep most of it onboard.

By the next morning, most systems seemed to be working normally again. Lacking energy to move I decided that I would stay for another couple of days before venturing to the mountains. I spent the day reading. Drinking tea. Had a small lunch. Read some more. Then I had dinner and went to bed.

The next day, I was feeling alive again. It was time to discover Gondar. One of the most interesting cities I've been to in Africa. From its ancient churches to Fasilides' castle which dates back to the late 1600s, everything about Gondar was fascinating.

The next morning, I checked out and headed for Debark. Home of the Simiens National Park office where I would be able to organise a guide and scout for my trip. The journey to Debark was made in a shared taxi, sitting next to a young female, Siti, who made sure the taxi driver did not overcharge me. She also made sure that the taxi driver got me onto another taxi at the halfway stop and that they did not overcharge me. Proof that angels exist. Everywhere.

From the accounts I'd read about trekking here, and the pictures I had seen, I'd been wanting to visit the Simien Mountains in Ethiopia for a few years now. I expected some stunning mountain scenery. But I wasn't anywhere near prepared for the endlessly dramatic peaks and rolling hills that unfolded in front of me as I trekked from the Sankaber area to the top of Ras Dejen and back to Chennek. Ever since I've visited the Simiens, I've been telling people that they were like the Drakensberg – only 1000 metres taller. Then, while writing this, I came across the following on Wikipedia:

> *"Because of their geological origins, the mountains are almost unique, with only South Africa's Drakensberg having been formed in the same manner and thus appearing similar."*

After I parted with the right amount of money for my summit trip – five days' worth of park and scout fees, I was assigned a scout and a guide. Paying five days fees when I could potentially have climbed the mountain in two days, irked me. But I thought better than to complain to the local clerk who took my money, who did not set the rules.

The scout was a weathered 74-year-old of Islamic background. 'Shah' Hosseini carried a Lee-Metford gun that was even older than he was and followed me everywhere like a shadow, without missing a single step. A totally lovable character. I gave him my poncho during the trip, to keep him dry when it was raining and add a layer of warmth. He hugged me like a brother, with tears in his eyes. The communication between the two us needed no words.

The guide's name was Jijaw. A young chap, with a fantastic knowledge of the plants and animals we encountered on our trek. We had a minor hiccup along the way. Jijaw did not contact the shuttle service I had asked him to organise for our return journey, which meant we spent an extra day in the mountains. After a beer or two, and a chat, the incident was forgotten about.

Jijaw recruited a cook for the trip. A man I would happily cross the continent with. Yrga. Cook extraordinaire. Ex-soldier who had seen service in Sudan, Eritrea, and elsewhere. A gentle soul, with a great sense of humour and an ability to cook a scrumptious meal with a single primus stove and lots of enthusiasm.

He also organised another local guide to provide transport to the start of the walk. This is how I came to meet Abera, who has become a good friend. Abera picked us up the next morning. After a short stop-over to have a look at Jin Bahir falls, where I was treated to a magnificent aerial display by a griffon vulture, we stopped at a village near Sankaber. We hired two muleteers and their mules to transport our tents, food, and spare clothing. Abera dropped us a few kilometres further. Jijaw, Shah Hosseini and I set off for Geech. Arriving at Geech the team started setting up camp. With tents pitched, and Yrga the cook getting busy in the field kitchen, Jijaw, Shah Hosseini and I set off for a walk to the escarpment edge. A troop of gelada (*Theropithecus gelada*) are known to spend time here before retiring to their sleeping area. Sometimes called gelada baboons, these ape-like creatures are in fact not baboons at all, but the only living species of the genus *Theropithecus*.

Geladas spend their nights sleeping on ledges on cliffs, where they are safe from predators. Daytime is spent feeding and socialising. Ninety percent of the gelada's diet consist of grass: eating both the blade and the seed. This makes them the only primates that are primarily *graminivores* (seed eaters). When available they dig roots and rhizomes with their hands. They also eat flowers, herbs, fruits, thistles, and other small plants when available. Insects are also eaten when easily obtainable.

Researchers from the University of the Free State in South Africa observed that some gelada females 'cheat' on the dominant male partner. They would mate with a non-dominant male, suppressing the normal mating cries so as not to be discovered. If discovered the non-dominant male would be punished by the dominant male. These observations led the researchers to believe that dishonesty is not a uniquely human trait. And that the human system of dishonesty and punishment started long before we started walking on two legs.

While I was sitting and observing these fascinating creatures, we were joined by another party who had made camp at Geech. One of whom was to be our future companion on Mount Stanley and Mount Kenya.

On our way back to the campsite, Jijaw and I spotted the very rare and shy Ethiopian wolf (*Canis simensis*). Earlier we also had come across antelope, numerous species of smaller birds, a griffon vulture, sacred ibis, a bearded vulture, an augur buzzard, and a pair of thick-billed ravens. I was impressed with the number of animals and birds we're encountering on our way and mention this to Jijaw. He explains that any person caught poaching either animals or bird gets locked up for twenty-four months. Another factor may be that the few people living in the national park are being resettled outside the park borders.

Back at the camp Yrga, the ultimate professional, is dressed in white uniform, and giving orders left right and centre. Get water. Bring this. Do that. Popcorn is served as a pre-dinner snack. While Yrga is cooking Jijaw takes a walk to the nearby village and hands the local teacher one of the soccer balls I had brought along. Rather than a few pens, which can't be shared by everyone, I thought a football would be a nice token of thanks for letting me walk on their paths. (I had also brought a box of pens, but these I'll hand to individuals or small groups that we encounter along the way.)

Dinner, a feast fit for a hungry hiker, is served with *injera* – an Ethiopian speciality. A spongy fermented flatbread with a slightly sour taste, traditionally made of teff flour. Then it's off to bed.

Day two breaks with a few clouds hovering about. After breakfast we set off for Imet Gogo, a 3947m high prow jutting out from the main escarpment from where the views across the mountain is absolutely amazing. Mandy and her team arrive a little later. They're not planning on going to the summit of Ras Dejen and will be heading back after today. I suggest that she would be welcomed to join our party if she wants to go to the summit.

While we're sitting and talking, I also mention that this trip is part of my preparation for climbing Africa's three highest mountains. Mandy asks if she can join us on the Mount Kenya leg, if her timing coincides with ours.

We leave and push on towards Chennek. At about midday, having reached the highest point of today's walk we stop for lunch. A welcome break from the energy sapping walking, most of which is taking place above the 3600m level. A height at which altitude sickness becomes a reality for many, and oxygen intake is reduced to about sixty percent of the volume you pull into your lungs at sea level.

Having started the hike at a fairly high altitude, I was fortunate not to have suffered from altitude sickness. Mainly thanks perhaps to the acclimatisation climb I had done a few weeks earlier to the summit of the 4167m high Jbel Toubkal.

But that did not make the walking any easier. With every step that I took, my lungs screamed for oxygen. My chest felt as if it was compressed with a straitjacket preventing me from breathing, and on top of that it felt like I was dragging a ton of lead on each foot.

It was probably about here that doubt, the satan that promotes failure, started singing its monotonous little tone: 'you're not going to make it to the four-thousand-five-hundred metre high summit…'.

On our way from our lunch spot we come across a flock of spurfowl. Brilliantly coloured, and perfectly blending into the yellow-gold coloured grass. They were foraging for food along the ridge we were following towards Chennek.

Spurfowl – Erckel's I think

Harry Loots

A little further on we come across four children who were selling handmade baskets. What were they doing up here, I'm wondering to myself? Did someone mention the mzungu that's trekking from Geech to Chennek, and they came up this way to make sure they were the first ones I encountered. Giving them a better chance at a sale? I happily parted with a few Ethiopian birr in exchange for one of the little baskets, even though I had no idea what I was going to do with it on my trek...

Four Ethiopian Highlands children selling handmade baskets

The campsite at Chennek is sited close to the Community Centre, offering accommodation, food, and drink. Mandy and her team are staying at the centre. We've pitched camp at the trekkers' campsite a few hundred metres away. I send Jijaw to buy the team a couple of beers each. And a fizzy drink for Shah Hosseini who does not drink any alcohol.

Mandy and I chat some more. She's decided that she can't fit the extra days going to the summit into her travelling plans. So, will be returning with the rest of the group to Gondar the next day. We exchange numbers and I promise to let her know dates for our Mount Kenya trek.

The team have pitched my tent inside the rondavel, suggesting it will be warmer here than outside. They've also made a roaring fire, which produces a lot of smoke, but also some very welcome heat to stave off the cold. Not happy with the fire and the tent in the same area, I get them to break down the tent, and opt to sleep on my mattress against the furthest wall away from the fire.

The first part of our next day's trek is somewhat boring following a road from Chennek to Chiro Leba. I manage to flag a goods truck down, and after parting with a thousand Ethiopian birr we jump on the back and ride the rest of the way to Chiro Leba.

Lunch – injera and a meaty sauce

Lunch is a drawn-out affair at a roadside café. The cooking happens in a tin shack, while the diners take refuge from the sun and rain under a makeshift awning consisting of four eucalyptus poles and some plastic draped over the top. After my experience a few days ago I'm wary of eating injera straight off the serving plate, so I opt for something safer. The team however thoroughly enjoy their café-bought lunch and the drink.

After lunch we set off for Ambiko, where we'll spend the night. Along the way we come across a priest and his small band of followers travelling in the opposite direction. As he passes by people kneel and give money to his band of followers. As I look at this charade, I'm left wondering how this priest whose demeanour is more like a rock-star than a disciple of the church, got himself into this position…

When we cross a water stream, we stop to water the mules and have a short break. A group of children travelling come and talk with me. After a while I discover that my role in this interaction is to enable them to practice their English.

They ask questions, and I respond. When they hear an unfamiliar word, they repeat it until they get the pronunciation right. With lots of laughter when they mess it up, and proud smiles when they get it right.

When the mules have been watered, Jijaw says we should go, but I tell him to hang on for a while I play language teacher. He sends the muleteers off with our equipment and settles down to act as interpreter when I am not able to explain the meaning of a word.

Before we set off, I give the children a ballpoint pen each. With happy smiles, they go off in their direction, while we continue up the narrow mule track. As we make our way up the mule-track I can hear their voices below repeating the new words they learnt. Little things mean a lot…

Shortly after we arrive at the campsite, on the edge of a village, Yrga serves us coffee and popcorn.

The cooking facilities are rudimentary compared to the previous days. An uneven piece of ground in a shelter constructed with eucalyptus poles. But that did not stop Yrga from producing yet another feast.

Jijaw and I chatting and enjoying our coffee and popcorn

After dinner I make myself comfortable on the slightly sloping floor of my tent, read a few chapters of my book, and then go to sleep. With just a few worries about the next day's summit attempt…

Jijaw, 'Shah' Hosseini and I are up at 5am the next morning. We wash down some coffee and baked bread, and then we're off. Jijaw is carrying a torch the size of a motorbike battery, which swings in all directions and keeps catching my eyesight, both blinding, and irritating me. I give him my back-up head torch and ask him to put his torch away. Shah Hosseini does not have a torch. And does not seem to need one either.

The first nearly eight-hundred vertical metres is a continuous battle with mud as we follow paths trodden by sheep, goats, and cattle. The stuff looks like slimy wet concrete and keeps sticking to my boots. Forcing me to stop and scrape it off every hundred metres or so.

Then as we leave the cattle paths, and level out just below the 4000m mark, walking gets a little easier, and I begin to believe that we will reach the summit. Walking for the next few kilometres at this altitude, gives my lungs a chance to catch up with its oxygen intake and my legs to cast off the lead that was beginning to cling to them.

Another short steep climb sees us gaining hundred-and-fifty or so vertical metres, and then shortly after we gained some more, we can see the summit ahead of us. Shah Hosseini, my shadow up to this point, stopped here while Jijaw and I continued to the flat rocky outcrop which protected the summit. A few hundred metres further and we are the base of the outcrop, probably forty or so metres tall.

Scrambling up through easy rock, stopping regularly to catch my breath and making sure I was steady on the exposed edges, I suddenly found myself standing on a featureless, unexciting, and anticlimactic flat rock platform on which a concrete block had been set, the only sign that you were on top of the fifth highest mountain in Africa.

It did not matter. I had made it. I was on top of the fifth highest mountain in Africa. I have reached a height of 4550m for the first time in my life, and I was feeling strong and full of energy. Jijaw and I congratulated each other. Had water and some of the packed lunch Yrga prepared. Then we just sat around for a while. Looking at the scenery below. A bearded vulture flew overhead. I gazed in awe at its skill and manoeuvrability. Jijaw broke the spell when he said we should be heading back. Scrambling down, more relaxed now, we made our way back to where Shah Hosseini was waiting for the two of us. Then we started back towards Ambiko.

On top of Ras Dashen – 4550m

On our way down we came across a young chap selling bottles of Coca-Cola and other fizzy drinks. He kept them cool under a tiny stream of ice-cold mountain water. I bought Jijaw and I one each and a Lemonade for Shah Hosseini. As soon we had finished drinking our cold drinks, and handed the bottles back to this enterprising youngster, he dropped all of his supplies into a bag, and set off down the mountain. Probably happy with the bit of extra money with which he could buy a few essentials for the family. I stood in awe, watching him down the hill, thinking of how hard he had to work to earn the equivalent of a few cents. Had to climb a few hundred vertical metres, and wait for us for however long, simply to sell three bottles of cold drink!

We stopped at Ambiko, where Yrga was waiting for us with some very welcome lunch and hot coffee. After lunch and a short rest we continued back towards Chiro Leba, for our return journey to Chennek. We caught up with the mules at the watering point and Jijaw suggested I take a break from walking and ride on a mule. I protested at first, but he thought we could move quicker this way, and, in the end, I gave in. Riding a mule on a narrow track, with drops of a few hundred metres below you at times was perhaps not the most fun I've had. There were no reins to hold on to, so I had to hold on to the ropes securing the load. More than once I thought the mule and I were going to end up in the riverbed far below. But, despite my moments of worry, the mule seemed to know what it was doing, and carried both of us safely to the road.

It was at Chiro Leba village that I discovered Jijaw had not phoned for the transport to collect us that afternoon. And now he did not have a signal. All efforts to find alternative transport failed. There was nothing available.

Except for a three-wheeled tuk-tuk taxi, who was prepared to drive us to the head of the pass. From where we had to walk the rest of the way to Chennek. Arriving about the time that the hut guardian was clearing the dinner table. A few beers later, and after a warm dinner, and all was forgiven.

Instead of sleeping in the tent, Jijaw organised that I stay in the Community Centre. When I looked into the room where my bag and clothes had been deposited, I had a moment of worry about bedbugs, fleas, lice, and the like, but was too tired to make a fuss, and was asleep almost before my head hit the pillow. Woke the next morning with a body that felt it needed a rest, but not a single bite mark.

Later that morning Abera picked us up. Dropped Jijaw and company in Debark and organised a taxi to take me back to Gondar. The taxi driver decided he would try and charge me extra as soon as Jijaw and Abera had left. I handed over the sum we had previously agreed and made it clear that I'm not paying anything more than that. I got my way.

Two days later it was time to fly back to Nairobi. Abera picked me up from the hotel. Driving to the airport I saw a naked man walking down the road. I asked Abera about this man, and also remembered having seen a naked man sitting on the pavement in the middle of Gondar the day before. Both seemed completely at ease with their nakedness, even if not at ease with the world at large. The people passing them ignored them. Abera responded that they lived in an institution for sick people. That people accept them as they are. The endlessness of African tolerance. If this had been the UK there would have been three police cars screaming down, ready to take this 'offender' away.

I could bore you with pages and pages of what I did preparing for the trip. Which pee bottle I took, and which hand warmers I chose (don't make unnecessary connections here). Where I got maps from. Which guidebooks I consulted. What equipment I needed, what medicine I packed, which brand of whiskey we took along, etc., etc… I won't. If you need advice on equipment, email me. I'll try to help.

My gear, ready to go into bags

## FINDING GUIDES

I made two exploratory trips to Kenya and Tanzania. To find local guides that I felt I could trust and would be happy to work with on this huge adventure. I was getting too many yes responses from local guides. Even when no would have been the obvious answer. And thus not getting the level of confidence I needed in the guides/operators. Part of the problem being language. The other part of the problem being the desire of many people to provide the answer that will please the most.

Operators on Mount Stanley remained a mystery, right to the time we landed. But since there were only two operators who provided trekking services on the mountain, I only had a fifty-fifty chance of picking the wrong one. I picked one and arranged dates and times with them. They let me down a few weeks before the trip, by suddenly asking for more money for a trip they had already quoted for in detail. That simply meant they were the wrong choice. At which point it became a simple choice of getting a price from the other crowd. And having faith that they would not let us down as well. Which I'm happy to add, they did not.

Both exploratory trips turned out to be huge adventures in themselves. First stop was Kenya. I first climbed Mt Kenya in 2008. Arrived in Nairobi. Walked up to a tour provider, asked him to provide me with a guide. He made a few phone calls. And that's how I came to meet Moses. Moses and I became good friends. Moses and I kept in touch over the years. Whenever I visited Kenya, I'd make sure that I catch up with him.

This time however we were planning a trip for two people and I wanted certain structures in place. For example, multiple guides in case one of us had to drop out, so that the other could continue. We also recruited Duncan as the 'technical climbing guide'. I've known Duncan for a few years. But this would be the first time we would work together - the previous time having been cancelled due to massive political unrest in Kenya. With everything organised it was time to move on.

I decided to catch the night train to Mombasa. The last time I was on this train, the twelve-hour trip took about eighteen hours. But I did get to sit in the driver's cabin with the engineer and his assistant. Thanks to having dinner with them the night before and having worked as a train driver's assistant before starting my studies. Prime viewing position as the sun was rising across Tsavo. Elephant. Giraffe. Antelope, and views towards Kilimanjaro.

Sailing through African countryside on the now defunct 'overnight' train

The train broke down about three-quarters of the way, and after some time waiting in the field, a bus arrived and took us the rest of the way.

I helped an elderly couple carry their luggage from the train to bus and they gave me a medallion with the Canadian Maple leaf as a thank you. Much as I did not think I deserved a medal for helping them, I very much appreciated this gesture.

Despite the delay, I fell in love with this train. The 'olde world' atmosphere. Private first-class cabin. 'Air-conditioning' only working when the windows are open, and the train is moving. A rather erratic 'air-conditioner'. What with the windows getting stuck in either open or close position at the most inappropriate times.

Food freshly cooked on board and served in a proper dining car. Dinner a three-course affair. Chilled wine and cold beers; gin-and-tonic with a slice of lemon and ice. Stuff straight out of an African film set. So, I thought I'd do it again. Booked a ticket for Friday evening. Due to arrive in Mombasa Saturday morning by noon.

This time the trip only took thirty hours… Departure was delayed by nearly four hours. While sitting at the station, a Kikuyu lady asked if she could share the table. We started chatting. Rose, the Kikuyu lady was also going to Mombasa. To while away the time, I asked her how to say hello and please and thank you in Swahili. She proceeded to teach me a few basics.

The next morning at breakfast, the train was standing at a station. We found out that we have been delayed by about eight hours – cause guessed at. New ETA was now 17:00 – only five hours delay... We started moving. To the next station. And stopped. And waited. Walked around. Got back on board. Had a coffee. Walked around some more. A goods train came past going in the opposite direction. We started moving again. To the next station. Stopped. Waited. Walked around. Had a cold Tusker. Practised my Swahili. Then a train came past in the opposite direction. Finally we moved on.

It was now clear that the goods trains carrying high-quality cargo were being given preference to our train full of passengers. Which is probably the opposite of what would have happened in most western countries. But I am guessing that late running goods trains cost the railways penalties. While there were no penalties to pay to passengers… Our new ETA 20:00 – delay only eight hours. We got as far as the next station. Stopped. Waited. Walked around. Had more cold Tuskers. Practised more Swahili. Then it got dark. Had more cold Tuskers while waiting for dinner to be served. New ETA 01:00.

We finally arrived in Mombasa at about 3.30 a.m. Sunday morning. Thirty plus hours later. I asked Rose if she had accommodation and when she said no, I invited her to share my hotel room, which she gratefully accepted, given the hour. With a tinge of guilt I wondered what the few hundred other travellers would be doing this time of the night to get accommodation. For many it may well have been a night on the station platform, or at a bus stop somewhere waiting for the first bus to depart to wherever they were going next…

I was meant to go back to Nairobi on Sunday evening. On the overnight train. Then fly to Kilimanjaro International Airport the next day. Decided I wanted at least a day on the beach before heading for Tanzania. Cancelled the return journey and decided to go overland instead. One might have thought that after a thirty -hour journey one would have taken a flight…

So instead of packing to go back soon after I woke up, I spent the day exploring the area around Diani Beach. Later I went for a long walk and then relaxed on the beach.

The next morning Rose helped me to get on one of the local buses, which leave when they're full, unlike the mainline buses that leave at scheduled times. The white face amidst the sea of locals drew the usual attention – especially from little people onboard. Soon I was chatting to an elderly gentleman on his way to Nairobi.

Overtaking in the face of ongoing traffic seemed to be a speciality of this bus driver. More than once I found myself wanting to duck out of the way of an oncoming vehicle. I should add I was impressed how he managed to squeeze the bus into spaces that a Mini Minor would have had trouble fitting into.

Somehow, we made it to Voi, where I was dropped off. From here to Moshi, it's shared taxis. Matatus they're called. Which apparently comes from Swahili slang for 'three' – the original cost of the fare being three coins. I finally found a matatu and hopped on board. Once again, the only mzungu... a smiling mzungu who dozed off, only to be woken by Paul, who was sitting on my right, to show me the Giraffes next to the road. A very proud Paul, showing off 'their' animals. Paul was on his way to Taveta, the little town on the Kenya/Tanzania border, where he worked as a clerk in the local hospital.

It was nightfall when we got to Taveta. Too late to cross the border and get to Moshi. He suggested I stay at a local hotel he recommended. I accepted, and he walked me to the hotel. Paul introduced me to the receptionist who booked me into a room on the first floor. I invited Paul to join me for dinner. After I dumped my bag in my room, I joined him in the lounge. We ordered fish and chips – a local 'speciality'. Then I went to bed. Mosquito net draped over the bed to keep the little creatures out.

Woke up the next morning and had a shower. Whilst drying myself, I noticed a box on top of the television set – one of the four pieces of furniture in the room. The other being the bed with its mosquito net, a wardrobe, and the sideboard on which the television stood. Wondering what sort of box would be placed on top of a television set I pulled it down. Turned out to be a box of condoms. One-hundred-and-forty-four to be exact. Though it looked like there were more than a few missing. Never did find out if I was the only guest not renting the room by the hour that evening...

After breakfast I checked out and went looking for a taxi. I spotted a young chap on a boda-boda. Boda-bodas are cycle or motorcycle taxis. The word is borrowed from the Swahili word *bodaboda*. Meaning 'border border', the origin of the term is claimed to have come from Busia, a small trading village on the Uganda/Kenya border. Local traders would hire motorcycle taxis to transport goods from Kenya to Uganda, and so started this 'border to border' transport system. Today there are thousands of boda-bodas everywhere in East Africa. They're quick, convenient, and cheap. Even if it feels at times when you zip in and out of traffic, that you're passing very close to cars coming and going in both directions…

The young chap is happy to take me to the border, from where I can get a matatu to Moshi. I ask him if he can go beyond the border. He says yes. And so, after checking in at the border control, getting my yellow fever certificate and passport stamped, I walk through to Tanzania, jump on the back of the boda-boda and continue my journey into Tanzania. On the back of a motorcycle. At the next village he drops me off. After I paid him, he turns and heads back to Kenya. A little while later a matatu comes my way and I flag it down. I check that they're going to Moshi, and on getting confirmation, hop aboard.

The next morning, I made my way to the Coffee Union Café (mentioned in Lonely Planet and other tourist guides). I ordered a coffee and because they spoke good English, I asked if they knew any local mountain guides. They suggested I hang around for a while, as one of their regulars was a guide. A while later Ronaldo arrived. I took an immediate liking to him and knew that I had found the person who could help André and I get to the top of Kilimanjaro.

Roll forward to July 2016. After months (one might even say years) of planning, we are finally on our way to start our mammoth adventure: to climb Africa's three highest mountains.

It felt like I had come a long way from Platberg…

Mount Stanley is the highest of six massifs that make up the Rwenzori Mountains in Uganda. The third highest mountain in Africa. Mount Stanley consists of three peaks, the highest of which is Margherita Peak (5109m). It is the fifth highest peak in Africa after Kibo (on Kilimanjaro), Batian and Nelion (on Mount Kenya), and Mawenzi (also on Kilimanjaro). The next highest peak after Margherita Peak is Mount Kenya's Point Lenana and the next six highest peaks are all located in the Rwenzori Mountains.

In the 1980s authorities agreed to rename the 'Ruwenzori Range' to 'Rwenzori Mountains'. Rwenzori was considered to be closer to the original name 'Rwenjura', which means 'rainmaker'. And in case you're wondering why it changed from a range to a mountain… a mountain stands alone, while a mountain range is a chain of mountains. Which the Rwenzori is not.

The Rwenzori Mountains is made up of six massifs, separated by deep gorges and wide valleys. Mount Stanley, also known as 'Mount Ngaliema' (5,109 metres) is the highest, followed by Mount Speke (4,890 metres), Mount Baker (4,843 metres), Mount Emin (4,798 metres), Mount Gessi (4,715 metres), and Mount Luigi di Savoia (4,627 metres). Five of these massifs are listed among Africa's top ten highest peaks and each of the massifs consists of multiple peaks.

Straddling the equator, the Rwenzori extends for about hundred-and-ten kilometres from south to north along the border between Uganda and the Democratic Republic of Congo, and for about fifty kilometres east to west. It rises gradually from the Uganda side, but drops away dramatically and steeply on the western side to the Semliki or Semuliki River. The hundred-and-forty kilometres long river, which forms the border between Uganda and DRC, is the outflow of Lake Edward and empties into Lake Albert, one of the sources of the White Nile.

Though there are many crater-lakes found in the surrounding area, the mountain itself is not volcanic in origin, being the result of an upthrust that arose from within the western rift and which also divided paleolake Obweruka into the present-day Lakes of Albert and Edward.

Formed about three million years ago in the late Pliocene epoch, it consists of crystalline rocks: mainly gneiss, amphibolite, granite, and quartzite.

One of the first things you'll notice on the Rwenzori is the constant rush of water streams and rivers and the damp underfoot conditions. Wetter than her nearby East African cousins, the heaviest rainfall occurs on the eastern slopes facing the prevailing winds, and ranges from 2000 to 3000 mm depending on altitude. The wettest periods are from mid-March to May and again from mid-September to mid-December – the one feature that she has in common with her nearby cousins. André and I planned to be here in July, during one of the two dry periods of the year.

Thanks to her position on the equator the seasonal maximum daytime temperature does not change much. In the Alpine and Nival zones, daily air temperatures range between a minimum of -5 and a maximum of 20 °C.

In the boundary zone between the Bamboo and Ericaceous or heather zones, ranging from 3000m to 4000m, occasional night-time freezing may occur. Above 4000m freezing can be expected on 80-90% of nights.

Ancient Greeks told tales of mountains consisting of snow and ice being the source of the Nile. Aristotle referenced 'Mountains of Silver' as the source of the Nile. Claudius Ptolemy, a geographer, labelled the Rwenzori as "Lunae Montes" (The Mountains of the Moon), on his map published in c. 150. Despite these references, the mountains remained the stuff of legends. Sir Henry Morton Stanley had his first glimpse of the mountain in 1876. Confirming their existence. Later, in 1888 he saw the slopes of the mountain covered in snow.

Various parties made attempts to climb the mountain. They all failed thanks to the thick vegetation on its flanks, bad weather, disease, or lack of time. It won't be until 1906 that the Duke of Abruzzi would stand on top of Margherita Peak. The party consisted of six scientists, four alpine guides and more than three hundred porters, led by the Duke. They reached the summits of each of the six massifs. On 18 June 1906 the Duke, accompanied by J. Petigax, C. Ollier and J. Brocherel, reached the top of Margherita Peak, the highest point on Mount Stanley. He named the peak after his aunt, the Queen of Italy.

## Day 1: Travelling to Kasese

If you've never heard of Kasese, tucked away in the west of Uganda, close to the border with the DRC (Democratic Republic of the Congo), don't feel alone. Unless you are a local living in Kasese, work in the tourism industry in Uganda, are looking for work in the copper or cobalt mining industry, or you live in eastern parts of the DRC and need supplies that are not available in your country, you probably won't have heard of it either.

Boasting a population of about a hundred-thousand inhabitants, Kasese was built around the now near depleted copper mining industry, which has been kept alive only because cobalt is being extracted from the sludge, and for that a labour force is needed. Some five-thousand local people are employed by the mining industry which makes for a sizable chunk of the local economy. Given that only about five-hundred people walk the Rwenzori annually, tourism is probably a negligible factor in sustaining the local economy. Sadly, there's a high rate of malnutrition in the area, higher than the rest of Uganda, which leads to an increased incidence of stunted growth. According to a WHO report this is not necessarily due to lack of food. It seems that due to other factors, such as vegetables being fed to pigs and other livestock instead of being consumed, mothers spending their days trading the vegetables they grow at the markets to augment their income, and older siblings looking after smaller ones, who may not provide the same level of care and supervision as an adult might.

But if you were to walk along the streets or visit a local shop or market or anywhere else, you wouldn't be aware of this. The people are friendly, warm, and cheerful. Come the evening, the streets, reserved for business traffic during the day become a street food zone. The buzz is electric and the mood happy, and the food, ranging from roasted cob to chicken is cheap.

To get to Kasese you can fly to the local airport – at nearly the same price you would pay for a cheap economy ticket from Europe to Entebbe. Or you can use local buses. Or hire a taxi for about one-hundred-and-fifty US dollars one way, which if there are two or three sharing is probably the most convenient option. Not that it's much quicker. No traffic in Uganda is ever going to be quick. Deliberately slowed by sleeping policemen crossing the road every few kilometres and guaranteed to give you whiplash if you dare try to bounce across them at speed. That is if the thousands of potholes don't dislodge your spinal column from your neck bone first...

So, if you were expecting to travel the three-hundred plus kilometres in let's say typical times one would expect in Europe or the US, then think again. Double the time and you'll come closer to an estimated time to complete the distance. Despite being aware of the various drawbacks of travelling this way, André and I nevertheless opted to go by taxi. This was probably the sensible option as we could travel direct from Entebbe Airport to Kasese, without having to drag our luggage to the shuttle bus, which would have taken us into Kampala, then deposited us somewhere, from where we would have had to drag our luggage for who knows how long until we got to the bus stop from which the buses to Kasese departed...

Although more comfortable than a bus, it wasn't perfect, and by the time I got out of the car in Kasese, I had had enough of sitting in a car seat. But there was one more short journey to make to the Rwenzori Mountaineering Service's lodge very close to the National Park Gate before our travelling for the day was completed.

The local population did not appear to take notice of the fact that the track that brought us to the lodge was suitable for animal drawn carriages only, or perhaps even safer still, on foot, and along the mostly single-track pothole-strewn and eroded track we encountered all kinds of vehicles ranging from bicycles laden with goods twice the height of the bicycle, to the ever present boda-bodas (motorcycle taxis) which carried anything from live goats to two to three passengers, to trucks and buses carrying all kinds of goods and people… Along a single track 'road'. I say road with hesitation, given the condition of this track. But in places it was obvious that this road, in desperate need of some maintenance work serves a large community and is their main route into Kasese and beyond.

The owner of the taxi, Paul, did his best to dodge the potholes and manholes and deliver us safely to the lodge where Mandy had already made herself at home.

The same Mandy I had met in the Ethiopian mountains a month or so before coming to Uganda. I had mentioned our plan to climb all three of Africa's biggest mountains to Mandy. She was keen to join us on the Mount Kenya leg, and so we exchanged phone numbers and kept in touch. Then a few days ago I got a WhatsApp that she'll be in Kasese about the same time as André and me. At some point over the next day or so, Mandy decided that she was close enough to Kasese to make the small diversion and come and meet her two companions for the Mount Kenya leg of our adventure.

A few cold drinks and a simple dinner later, André and I convinced Mandy to join us on the Rwenzori leg, with the understanding that this may be at the possible risk of her skipping Mount Kenya…

Somewhat weary after more than thirty hours of near continuous travel we didn't hang about after dinner and were soon shown to our huts. I did not realise how stiff my back had become from sitting for the best part of thirty hours until I picked up my tog bag in the room and immediately went down like a sack of dropped potatoes. Muscles that had got used to being in a sitting position, were not ready to pick up 32kg of tog bag. My lower back muscles snapped like a rubber band and I found myself lying on the floor trying to catch my breath and wondering what had happened.

Perfect start to the expedition. A stuffed back. And I haven't even walked ten metres…

For the next couple of weeks, I discovered what having a sore back was all about. Sleeping was painful. Standing was painful. Sitting down was painful. About the only thing that wasn't painful was when I was walking once the back had warmed up. Ibuprofen became my very close friend.

Footnote: Possibly from adjusting my stride to compensate for the backache, I ended up with a trapped nerve. While the back was slowly but surely getting better, the trapped nerve seemed to be slowly but surely getting worse. Fortunately, I managed to dislodge this trapped nerve with yoga-like hip-stretch exercises, twisting and stretching through the pain, while lying on a cold hard floor in a Nairobi Hotel after we had returned from Mount Kenya.

## Day 2: Waking in the jungle

Sleeping with my curtains open meant I woke with daylight spilling in through the windows. Lying in my warm bed, I enjoyed the early morning call and chorus of the birds outside for a while, before getting up and stepping into the cold shower.

Feeling refreshed, I stepped out of my hut. Straight into the jungle. Tarzan himself would have been happy to call this home. Surrounded and dwarfed by giant trees, hanging vines, and waving palms, with the song of birds coming from every possible direction, led by the ever-present Bulbul, and the sound of water rushing down the river, it is tranquil and a perfect place to relax after thirty hours of near continuous travel… Towering above our camp, is the mighty Rwenzori. And although the presence of Africa's third highest mountain is tangible; she is living up to her reputation and almost completely obscured by mist.

Surrounded by jungle with the mountains beckoning

## Buying food for a small army

To be exact, that small army consisted of exactly sixteen people as we set off to buy food that afternoon with Jarom the tour operator's local organiser.

Those sixteen people consisted of André, Mandy, and I, two guides, a chef and a chef's assistant, plus nine porters (three porters each, agreed during dinner the previous evening with Jarom); i.e., sixteen people.

But perhaps, in Jarom's mind, even if we did not know this at the time, we were buying food for the nineteen people, including ourselves, that came down off the mountain? The three of us, two guides, a chef and a chef's assistant, plus now twelve porters (four porters each). Did we start with twelve porters, when we had agreed on nine? Did we pick up strays along the way who travelled with us? I don't know… But I do know that when we arrived back at the base camp, there were seventeen people in total present (Happy and his nephew scuttled off the day before, to attend the funeral of Happy's brother, who also happened to be the father of the nephew…)

Or perhaps, when looking at the pile of food we were amassing, we were buying food for the twenty-three people we 'discovered' had started up the mountain? Yes, apparently when we left Nyakelengeni there were twenty-three people in our party! That was André, Mandy, and me, plus: two guides, a chef and a chef's assistant, plus sixteen porters (that's now five-and-a-third porters per person).

What I do know is that there were nineteen people on the photograph I took at Nyabitaba Hut on the afternoon before we descended to the park's gates.

I discovered the extra four porters at about the time that we started the descent after a successful summit ascent, during a discussion with Josephat on how much it would be appropriate to tip the porters.

Josephat had a wealth of experience and endless knowledge of the mountains and plants, and without his assistance and support we would have been hard pushed to reach the summit. He also had a habit of coming up with long-drawn-out speeches, each one starting with how welcome we were on the mountain, and then some other niceties before continuing with the essence of the brief. In this case, the speech was the one about 'tipping-comes-from-the-heart-and-one-must-give-as-little-or-as-much-as-one-can-see-fit'…

This was when I discovered that the little army of nine porters, I thought we had hired, had become sixteen. Unfortunately for us, it was explained, one porter had taken ill on day two and three others supported him off the mountain, which meant that sadly we had fewer personnel to help us achieve our goals and of course we would have had a much better trip if the unfortunate four who had to depart after day one were able to stay with us for the duration… Personally, I thought we had managed just fine and had an excellent and successful trip to the summit! But apparently this was not the case; apparently, we would have had a far better trip and much greater success if the four missing porters had been able to stay with us…

The speech continued about how very unfortunate it would be for the four porters who had to return home, if they were not to receive the normal tip they could have expected at the end of the trip, as it was, of course, entirely beyond their control that they were not able to help us achieve our goals, and the tip would of course greatly help to support their families, and especially as they were definitely there to 'support us' for the duration (even if they were back at home from day two), we should of course also please allocate a tip for the four porters who returned home.

I genuinely couldn't see how we could not compensate these unfortunate fellows who would have loved to have helped us to the summit. I somehow expected that the four would be waiting for us when we returned to the lodge, where we handed out tips and said thank you to the team, to congratulate us and commiserate on our not having had the best possible trip to the summit, thanks to their absence.

Sadly, they were not able to attend the tip handover ceremony, either. Perhaps it was a family emergency. Or perhaps they were attending the funeral in the village. Or maybe they were helping another sick porter off the mountain. I can only guess as to why they were 'sadly, not able to make it'… And I never discovered the gallant gentlemen's names who sullied our success by their early departure, or whether the one who had taken ill, survived the ordeal. But I did hand over an additional bundle of notes, equal to four tips, to our guides. The tidy little sum was gratefully received by our guides, who promised to deliver it to the four porters the very next day...

Back to buying food for an army, and what turned out to be a total waste of a day for Mandy and I who accompanied Jarom into Kasese, among other things to draw cash to pay for our trips.

First, having been told we'd be picked up at 10am, Mandy and I were ready by about 10am. André went back to bed to catch up on some sleep lost during the travels to Kasese. At some point while we were waiting, the lodge keeper informed us that the 'free' taxi we had been promised, had left earlier, which meant we missed our opportunity to have the free ride. He could however now organise a different taxi, but we would have to pay for this taxi. No chance I was going to pay for a taxi at this point. We were quite happy to stay in Kasese but were told we could stay for free at the lodge, and a taxi would be provided. I made it clear that we would not be able to pay them upfront for the trip if we don't have a taxi into Kasese, and we would not be charged for this taxi.

The taxi eventually arrived. At about 1.30pm – only about three-and-a-half hours later than promised. With the same driver, we had the evening before. The same driver that had apparently left too early for us to go with him. Along the way to Kasese we had a few stops. I switched off to the interruptions at this point, and just let them happen. Resigned to the fact that we would eventually get to Kasese. Resigned to the fact that we would eventually buy food, and that we may get back to the lodge before tomorrow, when we were due to start up the mountain... Arriving in Kasese we were first taken to ATMs where we discovered that the local ATM had a limit on how much we were able to withdraw in a single day. Unable to draw the full amount due, between Mandy and I we were able to draw enough money from three different accounts and several different ATMs to pay sufficient of a deposit to enable us to proceed with the trip the next day. But only after an endless series of calls between Jarom and his managers to discuss whether our part payment is acceptable or not. At some point, after one of the many calls, Jarom turned to us and said that his managers would be okay with the deposit we supplied, but we'd have to leave our passports with them for security. I said no. A few phone calls later they agreed to accept our part payment now and receive the remainder of the funds when we return. Without keeping the passports. Which we all knew was going to be the outcome, two hours earlier when the phone calls started. But in typical Africa style the discussion and negotiation had to be turned into a multi-act drama. The script had to be followed to the letter to ensure the conclusion to the drama is reached not too soon. Thus, preserving that moment of satisfaction, the finale, when everyone finally agrees on the outcome, to the very last minute. It did however mean that Mandy and I had a whole day wasted. André, lucky bugger, meanwhile caught up on his sleep, and afterwards spent time reading his novel.

After traipsing from one ATM to the next to get enough cash to pay a deposit, then sitting and waiting while phone call after phone call was made and translated and followed up with another phone call with our response followed by another translation and discussion and followed by another phone call, we finally got around to the task we were meant to have done during the morning – we went shopping for food.

From one shop to the next we went. One sold us toilet paper, the next one sold us cooking oil, another one peanut butter, another one water, and bread, until eventually we had a small mountain of food waiting to be transported back to the camp with us. This was before we made our way to the fresh market for vegetables and fish.

One might have reasonably expected that this would be an organised process… i.e., from a shopping list devised by the chef, to cater for three trekkers, two guides, plus the chef and his assistant. (The porters cooked their own food.) For example, one might have expected Jarom to purchase x-number of bags of rice or pasta, x-number of chickens for x number of meals, enough fish for one meal, x-number of vegetables, x loaves of bread, x tins of coffee, x bags of tea, x litres of milk, etc, etc, etc… But, in practice this 'process' turned out to be more a case of 'do you like this?' and into the shopping bag it went. If Mandy said to Jarom she wasn't able to eat this or that due to food-allergies, Jarom thought the rest of us wouldn't be able to eat it either so it didn't go in the shopping bag. An alternative to whatever was 'deleted' from the 'shopping list' was not provided either, which in the end resulted in a poor selection of provisions and a shortage of food. Fortunately, we discovered this shortage early on, so we were able to send one of our porters back to base to return with additional supplies. And, in hindsight, we should have sat down with Jarom and the chef and agreed a menu and quantities before we set off to buy, but, we assumed, that as an experienced tour organiser he would know how much to buy. Ah well… Lesson learnt. And applied on our next leg.

Note: In the end, after the supplementary supplies were received, we had more than enough to eat – and tastefully prepared by our very capable chef, Happy and his assistant Ronald, which we learned earlier was Happy's brother's son.

## Day 3: Nyakelengeni to Nyabitaba hut (2652m)

*Time / distance / height-gain: 4-5 hrs, 10km, 1006m*

It's 07.20 and the first day of walking has arrived. I'm not particularly keen to throw the warm blankets off and get into a cold shower. A luxury by the way, as my next wash will probably be in an ice-cold mountain stream. That's if I'm lucky enough to be near a stream, otherwise it's going to be a couple of wet wipes doing their best to freshen up strategic places…

Three trips later, I have my earthly belongings lying in the eating hall, ready for sorting. After breakfast André and Mandy collect their gear as well and the big sort starts. We're allocated 12.5kg of personal equipment each, including the bag in which our gear will be carried, so some things will have to stay behind. Many things in fact, given that I came with a total of 43kg of equipment. Only a small proportion of which were cold weather gear Mandy asked me to get her in the UK. A sleeping bag rated to -15°C, base layers and warm jacket, thick socks – essential for staying alive at altitudes above 3000 m…

Climbing gear is set aside – we'll need these on Mount Kenya. Ice axe, crampons, boots, thick socks, extreme weather gloves, extra mid layers (top and bottom), all goes into the must-go pile. Underpants… mmmmm… three will have to do – one on, one in the wash – drying, one spare. (Standard mountaineering joke: wear them back to front after day one; then inside out after day two, and inside out back to front on day four to make them last longer). The same goes for t-shirts. One pair of shorts on. One pair of longs in the bag. Wet weather gear in. Thick woollen jumper in (I tried fleeces many years ago and decided to stick with wool). Sleeping bag and liner in. Small towel, toothbrush, toothpaste, soap, (Lush powder) deodorant in. Ibuprofen, Imodium, bandage, plaster – enough first aid. Mini tool with pliers in (fixes broken packs and all kinds of things). Pocket knife. Book. Half a dozen energy bars. Head lamp. Spare batteries. Notebook. Duct tape. All in about 9kg André and I estimate – the somewhat officious Mr Ronald, chief weigher, and recruitment officer, having left with the scales. Much to André's delight, that means I have spare capacity, and he won't have to carry his crampons and ice axe on his back…

About midday, Jarom arrives back with two guides, Josephat and Bosco. Apparently, Fred, who is an excellent guide, and who was specially chosen for our group, to make sure we have the best guide with us, had to take one of his children who had taken ill to the doctor, and so we are now apparently lumped with the not-as-good-as-Fred Josephat and Bosco. What an awful put-down for the two guys who have to guide us up this mountain, I thought, so responded with 'I'm sure we've now got the two best guides with us, many thanks.'.

At about 12.30 we finally have our 10.00 am departure… and less than ten minutes later we reach the gate where we sign in, pay our park fees, take a last look at the route we are about to undertake on the huge map on the wooden board at the gate, and then we're on our way. To conquer the mountain. Our first stop will be Nyabitaba Camp.

The walk through the beautiful rain forest is even better than any of us had expected. I ask Josephat about the name of a particular tree, and he takes that as an invitation to start telling us about various trees we encounter and their medicinal use. As we go along, we learn that this tree's leaves are used for headache, and this one's leaves can be used if you have a cough. This one's bark can be put on a bleeding wound, and this one's leaves are used when we circumcise a boy [to stop infection]. There's even one that will make you more 'stronger' if your wife should be looking at another man, so that she will no longer have desires for the other man (and no, the leaves were not blue…).

The scenery is spectacular. We're surrounded by forests that seem to go on and on. Most of the day we're walking high above one river or another. Waterfalls abound. The one bigger than the other. The sound of the rushing river accompanied by a myriad of birds is a perfect soundtrack to our walking along this green lush stage.

Less than three hours later, and much to our surprise, having been told it's a four-to-five-hour walk, we reach Nyabitaba Camp. Which turns out to be a rather large hut with enough sleeping space for a few trekking parties, straddling the ridge we've been walking along. The simple wooden hut supported by stilts boasts wash basins, an outside flushing toilet and a cold shower. Surprise. Luxury. Right outside our door a sight to warm every South African's heart: a magnificent African yellowwood (Podocarpus latifolius). Majestic and with an aura of grandeur about it.

We spend the afternoon chatting among ourselves and getting to know our guides and porters – or at least the ones that can speak some English…

Then, after a simple scrumptious dinner, we are joined by our two guides, Josephat and Bosco, and Happy our chef for our nightly briefing about the next day's trek. The briefing always started with a long introduction about how welcome we are to the mountains and then continued with information about the next day's trek. We were told that we will be wearing rubber boots the next morning… At which point our guides discovered that some people have other ideas. Which does not include wearing rubber boots. We compromised by charging one of the porters with the duty of carrying the rubber boots should we need them en route. While I remained happy wearing my sandals, and getting my feet covered in mud occasionally as we made our way through the bogs, André, and Mandy, when they finally started wearing rubber boots, were of the opinion that they should have worn them from the outset. The thin soles, which made for a very hard contact with the ground underneath your feet, did not suit my pace, and I would opt for sandals every time over the rubber boots.

Expecting a much longer and tougher walking day ahead, we set off for bed. I wake in the middle of the night and make my way outside to heed the call of nature. The toilet is reached via a ramshackle wooden contraption which serves as stairs which I decide I'm definitely not attempting to negotiate in the middle of the night… A pee over the balcony edge into the bushes below will have to do.

Above me is a canopy of brilliant sparkling stars, outlining Portal Peak and reminding me just how much I miss the beautiful African night skies I grew up under.

## Day 4: Nyabitaba to John Matte (3414m)

*Time / distance / height-gain: 5-7 hours, 7km, 762m*

Breakfast. An omelette big enough to feed a small family each plus fruit arrived at our table and oats porridge to follow. This was exactly what we had asked them not to do.

All we had asked for was a bowl of oats each and some fruit for breakfast. None of us keen to start a day's hike on an overloaded stomach, the omelettes were sent straight back with instructions to wrap it in foil for us to take along as lunch.

Shortly after nine we set off up the ridge with glimpses of rivers, cataracts, and waterfalls, through gaps in the forest that we're walking in. After a few hundred metres, we start downhill towards the first of today's river crossings. A very sturdy steel suspension bridge with magnificent views up and down the river.

On the other side we stop to wait for the porters to pass us. As André steps aside on the path to allow a porter to pass, the patch of earth he had stepped on disappears, and so does he. Straight down into the undergrowth below. Fortunately, he doesn't fall very far, and apart from a few grazes, which Bosco and I patch up, he's okay.

Soon we're back on track, heading upwards, into more forest. Along the way we stop for more explanations about the medicinal uses of plants. This one's leaves can be used for a chest infection and this one you give your wife if she wants to divorce you to make her love you and not leave....

Harry Loots

At some point we walk through an area where bamboo grows – the 'bamboo region' according to our guides. (Given the size of the bamboo patch, I'm sceptical, but it turns out as we will see later, that they were 100% correct.) Then follows a few heather brushes. The 'heather zone'. The scenery, despite my scepticism at the 'zones', which is now constantly changing, is stunningly beautiful.

At our briefing the night before we were told that we'd be walking about four to five hours to the first resting spot. I thought that sounded like we're in for a tough and long stretch after breakfast and until we refuel.

To our surprise and delight the resting spot materialised less than three hours after we left Nyabitaba. A drink of water and a few minutes later we put our packs on to continue. Much to the surprise of our guides, who may have hoped for a much longer chat among themselves. On to the lunch spot we go, which turns out to be far enough away from our rest stop to make us all realise that we should have had lunch at the stop. And then followed one of those silly little short walks that make you wonder why you stopped in the first place for lunch when another half an hour would have brought you to the hut… Suggesting that the urge for an early start was unnecessary and a more leisurely start would have been perfectly okay, with lunch taken at the rest spot.

Needless to say, we're at the hut much, much earlier than the guides suggested we would be. Wondering how we can fill the next six hours before we go to bed…

Sometime during this long afternoon, Mandy went to the kitchen to get some hot water for tea and discovered that we had little in the form of meat / protein to go with our dinners and a huge oversupply of potatoes and rice. Not keen to summit a 5000+ metre mountain on starch alone, we decided that we'd have a meeting with our happy chef, Happy, later that day.

Making it clear from the outset that we're not looking to blame anyone, but that we're trying to resolve the issue and that we think he's a great chef we set about to map out a series of menus for the next five nights. (We should have done this before the trip. But expected our tour organiser would have had this in hand.) Once we had a practical menu for the next five days, we looked at what supplies we had and tried to figure out the gaps. Having identified the gaps we made a list which we were going to send back to base the next morning with instructions to please obtain and send with porters the supplies we needed and meet up with us at a hut two days hence.

To this list we decided to add one bottle of red wine to be shared the evening after we've summited Margherita Peak.

Having sorted out the menu and supply list, it was time for the briefing, which started with a warm 'welcome to the mountains'…

## Day 5: John Matte to Bujuku Camp (3962m)

*Time / distance / height-gain: 4-6 hours, 6km, 548m*

Clear skies as we wake and a drastic drop in temperature, making you almost wish for cloud cover… Then the sun breaks through. Breakfast arrives. Just oats and fruit this morning. Fruit that looks like it's been glazed. It's a step in the right direction. Tomorrow it will be perfect. It's warmer outside, so we enjoy our oats in the sunshine.

Very soon after leaving the hut we come to the first of the bogs. Lower Bigo Bog. Josephat tells that the bogs were much deeper once and that their forefathers tell a story of how someone fell in the bogs in the 1970s – never to be seen again. He also explains how they'd jump from tussock to tussock before the duckboards were installed. The vegetation is now changing from forest to heathland / moorland.

Senecios, Lobelias, Helichrysum and Giant Heathers have replaced the lush green forest.

Grasses, tussocks, and bogs

As we reach the head of the Bujuku Valley at about 3900m the effect of the altitude is beginning to make itself felt. The legs feel a little heavier and every once in a while, you have to catch your breath... The lake comes into view, and soon we catch a glimpse of the Bujuku Camp perched above.

But before we can get there, we have to navigate our way through muddy marshes. I'm still wearing sandals and after a few steps realise that no matter how I try I'm going to end up with mud on my feet. So, I stop caring about it and start enjoying traipsing through the mud on our way to the hut. My two compatriots though decide after this last few hundred metres through the mud that they will be wearing gumboots the next day.

Circumnavigating Lake Bujuku

Approaching the hut, I notice a mzungu sitting on a bench outside the hut. As I get nearer, I realise he's sketching. Thomas is from Stuttgart and his hiking companion Jens is from Nuremberg. They'd been at the hut since the day before, taking photos and in Thomas's case, sketching. And we would catch up with them again after our summit attempt.

Mandy and I decide to make the most of the sunny afternoon. We take up position next to the tiny stream that flows past the hut and soon I'm dozing off... André meanwhile decides to explore the ridge above and ends up going all the way to the head of the pass. As soon as the sun disappears behind the mountain above it starts getting cold – much colder than the preceding days. Possibly a combination of the higher altitude as well as the clear skies which results in a much higher inversion rate. Soon after dinner I crawl into my sleeping bag – tonight with my long-johns on – and not for the last time...

During my nightly trip, dictated by my
bladder, I find myself getting wet very
quickly from a relatively hard rain as I
step off the veranda of the hut. Logic
telling me that the pee will wash away
during the night, I decide not to run to
the toilet-hut, but instead to pee over the
side of the balcony (this is becoming a
habit). Getting back into my sleeping
bag turns out to be a massive battle
between me and the zip, with the zip
nearly winning as it tries to rob me of
every last ounce of breath, which seems
to be in desperately short supply now. Fortunately, I fall asleep quickly.

## Day 6: Bujuku Camp to Elena Hut (4541m)

*Time / distance / height-gain: 3-4 hours, 3km, 579m*

André and Mandy are up before me today. I hear Mandy saying to
André that it's snowed. I'm thinking Uh-oh, this could make our next
stage fun... Soon I'm out of my sleeping bag and into my warmest
clothes. Outside, the few inches of snow are already starting to melt.
One look at the snow + mud combination outside makes me decide to
become part of the gumboot brigade.

I had agreed with Josephat the evening before that we will take this leg
of our journey slowly. With neither of my two companions having been
to this altitude before I thought it sensible to break up the walk into
three stages with sizeable breaks at each stop. With Happy we organised
snacks and drinks for each stop. This would allow us to gradually gain
the nearly 600 vertical metres and to give our bodies the maximum
chance to acclimatise as we're ascending.

Our first break comes after about an hour, and for this break I've organised tea and chapatis for ourselves and our guides and chefs, to force us to sit down and have a proper break.

Amon, who looked after me and my equipment

As we get higher the snow is getting thicker and the vegetation is becoming more and more Alpine. At our second break we dig into our lunch packs: boiled eggs, cheese, and pro-vitas, for the third day in a row. It comes at just the right time, too, with my stomach beginning to moan loudly.

And then it's onto the last leg, through steep rocky terrain where we have to scramble from time to time.

We're at 4400+ metres. Higher than either André or Mandy have ever been. We're all feeling the strain of the altitude. Every breath is becoming more precious. Every step just a little heavier. The sight of the hut helps to motivate us to make the last few hundred metres, and we all collapse quite happily onto our hard bunks for a few minutes to catch our breaths.

Luckily not one of us, despite the advanced altitude, show any signs of altitude sickness. Meanwhile, outside our A-frame, Happy the cook is battling with the gas burner. I eventually take over from him and take the burner apart trying to clear the ducts but can't get it unblocked. Eventually concluding that the fault is in the pressure adjuster for which we'd need specialised tools to open it. Fortunately, there's another group on the mountain at the other operator's camp below us, and they can lend Happy some charcoal. We won't have to go hungry the night before we attempt to summit. Another lesson learnt for later: check if the chef has spares of critical equipment.

After dinner we discuss our departure time for the next morning. André wants to go at 4am, the time suggested by the guides, which doesn't suit either Mandy or I, both of us being unable to function in extreme cold. With the guides not being able to provide any reason why we should start at 4am, we eventually settle on a 5am start, so that our climbing time in the dark with headlamps would be limited. In hindsight, if I were to do this again, I would probably leave even later, do the scrambling in early daylight, and possibly try to do one of the other summits on the way.

Sometime during the night, I venture outside. Above us the stars are beautiful and bright. In the valley below an electric storm is raging. All I can see, being above the clouds is a disco effect, like the glow of coloured torches popping at a distance. When I feel my fingers getting cold, I head back to the warmth of my sleeping bag.

# Day 7: Summit day. Elena hut to Margherita peak (5109m)

*Time / distance / height-gain: 5-7hrs, 2.3km, 568m*

At about 4.30am Josephat comes into our hut to wake us. I think we were all awake already. Happy comes in with coffee and lunch packs. We all said no to breakfast at 4.30 in the morning. We eventually get going at about 5.30. Headlamps on we scramble up the boulder strewn valley that will take us up to the Stanley glacier. It's slow-going having to find a route through the maze of boulders with only headlamps. Some way up I call for a toilet stop. With my companions waiting twenty metres away, I do my bit to fertilise this barren rock-strewn part of the mountain. And with used toilet paper stuffed into a zip lock plastic bag for disposal back at the camp I re-join them, and we continue. No place to hide and very little privacy while on a climb…

We have no trouble hiking across the Stanley glacier and soon we scramble down and across the large boulders that now separate the Stanley and Margherita glaciers. Not too many years ago, most of this area was still under cover of the now retreating glaciers.

At 08.11 we are ready to tackle the final obstacle: the Margherita glacier. Unlike Stanley, this isn't a simple walk. With various near vertical climbs and a few hair-raising traverses above some very exposed drops, it's not a place for hikers. We rope together for safety. Which means we must move together. Which means progress is slower than before. You have to constantly watch the person in front so that the rope between you doesn't tighten to the point where if they move up, you'll pull them back, and they fall, and also the person behind to make sure you don't move too fast and pull them off-balance. And then there's the altitude factor. We're now at about 4800m. Your oxygen intake is now down to less than sixty percent of the oxygen available at sea level. Breathing, walking, even chewing your energy bar is an effort at this altitude.

The terrain has changed from easy scrambling across rock boulders and upright walking across snowfields, to steep inclines where your crampons are necessary for a firm foothold, and an ice axe shaft end driven into snow provides upright stability. These steep inclines are further interspersed by vertical sections of three, four, five metres in height, where ice climbing techniques must be used to move upwards. Here ice axes and crampons are no longer just for balance and grip, but they play an active role in your upwards movement, with  the front ends of crampons being firmly kicked into the ice to provide stable footholds, and the sharp end of the axe being driven into the ice to provide a handhold. Going is slow in the vertical sections, especially for Mandy who has never walked in snow with crampons, let alone climbed on ice.

The process of moving upwards on ice is relatively simple. Almost mechanical. First, you drive the sharp end of the axe into the ice, about six to eight inches above your head. This is your handhold. Then you drive the front ends of your crampons into the ice while holding on to your ice axe handhold. Then you move one crampon, six to eight inches higher. Then the next. And then you repeat. Ice axe upwards, driven into the ice, six to eight inches higher, crampons, one at a time six to eight inches higher, you move up until you reach the top. At the next vertical section, the process is repeated.

Horizontal sections, where you have to traverse across, are a bit more challenging. You chip a hole about waist high, place the axe end of the ice-axe into this hole with the shaft resting against the vertical wall, thus forming a stable handhold. Your leading hand goes on top of the axe both pushing down and in, to ensure the axe stays in place, and then you move your feet across about six to eight inches at a time. All the while with a vertical drop below you.

No wonder Mandy who had never climbed on ice before wanted to cry and/or throw up at this point. She did neither. Tears might have melted her 'handhold' and the rest would have turned the traverse into a slippery mess. Fortunately, this movement is done with a belayer at each end providing security should you lose faith in your equipment and fall. With Bosco on one end, and me on the other end, we belay Mandy across one little bit at a time. Then it's my turn to go across. Bosco belays me and I move as quickly as I can to get to the other side. The last steep incline beckons. Josephat is in front and leading at a slow pace so that the rest of us can keep up. Fifteen, twenty, thirty steps. Rest. Repeat. Until we reach the final rock band, above which beckons the summit.

Crampons off, we proceed with our day packs only, reaching the summit at about 10.45, about five hours and fifteen minutes after we left Elena hut. Not as quickly as we could have, but given the inexperience on ice in the team, not too long either. Most importantly we've made it. Safely. And we're on top of the third highest mountain in Africa. And the highest mountain in both Uganda and the Democratic Republic of the Congo.

Though the valleys below are covered with clouds, the surrounding peaks are basking in sunlight. It's lunch pack time. Two boiled eggs, cheese, and pro vita biscuits. Plus, a thick chapati. And fresh mountain water. Josephat and Bosco don't seem to be carrying lunch, so I give my chapati and egg to them with André donating one of his boiled eggs as well.

Bosco, Josephat, Mandy and André on Margherita Peak

## Descent from Mount Stanley

Apart from Mandy slipping and pulling me off a vertical section, with me getting the opportunity to practice an ice axe self-arrest, the descent is without incident and at about 15.30 we're back at Elena hut. André's first stop is the toilet, proclaiming proudly as he joins us at the hut that his day was perfectly planned, with a visit to the toilet immediately before departure and one immediately after arrival. Unlike my toilet stop halfway up the rocks…

Almost as soon as we drop our tired bodies down Happy brings out lunch. A simple lunch of rice and mix veg stew. My body isn't ready for any food, so I have a few bites to show appreciation. Shortly after we push off for lake Kitandara and the hut by the same name.

# Descend to Kitandara hut (4023m)

*Time / distance / height-loss: 2-3 hrs, 6km, 518m*

Amon and I reach Lake Kitandara with enough sunlight left to appreciate the reflection of the sunlit rocks towering above the lake. The hut is situated on the lake shore, with great views across the lake and beyond. André and Mandy with Josephat and Bosco arrive about half an hour later. Tired but elated. Early to bed is the call. But it's not until about 8pm that our dinner arrives. Mainly thanks to the fact that the replacement gas burner has not arrived. We eat and go to sleep...

View across Lake Kitandara

## Day 8: Kitandara hut to Guy Yeoman (3505m)

*Time / distance / height-loss: 5-6hrs, 5.8km, 518m*

I'm up and out early – taking a walk around the lake; snapping pictures as I go along. Happy is getting our breakfast ready with equipment borrowed from other parties. For the first time since we summited yesterday, I actually feel hungry. It's also the first meal since yesterday, that I don't feel ready to expel straight after eating it.

Our intended overnight stop is Guy Yeoman Hut. But after the day Mandy and I wasted when we went into Kasese, I'm particularly keen to get back closer to the main gate, so that we can hike out to the roadhead the next morning, to enable us to get taxis etc in place before another day is wasted in an endless waiting game. Getting back to Kasese would also allow us to settle in our hotel, do some laundry, and relax before we set off the next day for an eight-hour drive to Entebbe.

To achieve this, we would have to skip Guy Yeoman, and trek a further two to three hours to Nyabitaba.

Mandy agrees with me. André, perhaps having been spared the mindless time-wasting that Mandy and I had to endure, preferred staying overnight in Guy Yeoman. We all agreed to discuss this again when we arrived at Guy Yeoman.

And just in case you had skipped this part earlier, let me remind you of how our time was wasted... The 10am taxi arrives three-and-a-half hours later: at 1.30pm. Endless calls ensue between Jarom, the local tour organiser, and the tour company management to discuss our part payment. Agreement after several hours to accept our part payment now and receive the remainder of the funds when we return.

We finally started shopping for food about 4pm in the afternoon. One shop for oats, pasta, and a few other items... the next for water...

another for this... another for that... one market stall for potatoes... the next for cabbage... another for fish... and another for chicken... Finally, arriving back at the lodge as the sun was setting.

## The walk to Guy Yeoman

Our walk this morning is along a sometimes very steep downhill, partly equipped with wooden and metal ladders and staircases. As we progress down the hillside, the countryside gradually changes from a sub-alpine heather-filled habitat, to one filled with giant lobelia forests, artfully decorated, in a 'shabby chic' manner, with Old Man's Beard giving it an appearance of being both aged and ageless, and forests of everlasting shrubs and the constant sounds of sunbirds. Amon and I are again out in the lead. About 11-ish we stop for a 'lunch' break, with our lunch packs containing the now standard boiled eggs, cheese, and pro-vitas as well as a fruit.

Having been coming downhill through some bogs and very muddy and steep patches my hands are covered in black mud. While you're moving you don't think about the colour of your hands. But, while peeling my hard-boiled egg, and watching the pristine white of the egg become blacker and blacker I suddenly realised how muddy my hands had become. I took one look at the egg, vaguely wondering if I should wipe it with a wet tissue or something. Then popped it into my mouth.

Arriving at Guy Yeoman at about 1.30pm, I again ask the question about moving on, and again Mandy wants to move on. André has now decided he wants to stay at this hut because he likes the setting.

Knowing the hassle and amount of time it takes to organise taxis etc, I say I'll go down with a porter, so that at least one of us can be at the lodge early to order taxis and make arrangements for our onwards travel. I also decide that since I'm on my own and not to cause a massive rearrangement of staff, finding a 'cook' from among the porters, deciding which porter goes, etc, I'll push all the way through to the lodge, about six hours walk away, and not overnight at Nyabitaba, three hours away. As I'm packing my bag, André changes his mind, and we all set off for Nyabitaba.

## Guy Yeoman to Nyabitaba hut (2652m)

*Time / distance / height-loss: 2-3hrs, 6.6km, 853m*

The walk is pleasant enough and this time we actually find the bamboo region I had dismissed as being a gimmick on the way up. The change from lobelias to bamboo is welcome, and Amon and I spot a few Turacos plus some unnamed LBJs (little brown jobs for the initiated).

A few river crossings later we arrived at Nyabitaba. All three of us are ready for the cold showers that are on offer.

André and Mandy get into the showers first, while I start lining up the porters for a group shot. With much laughter, I get them arranged, and call André and Mandy to come and join us.

The team that heped us get to the top of Mount Stanley

André has finished showering and is busy dressing. Mandy however is still downstairs in the shower. Unbeknownst to her, I had lined up the entire team (minus the unknown four), ready for a picture.

We call her, and she makes her way upstairs, only to discover as she emerges at the top of the stairs, towel wrapped around her, that she has a whole gang of porters, chef and guides waiting for her... A quick dash into the hut and shortly she emerges. This time with something a bit more appropriate for a group photo.

I take a few group shots, and afterwards we treat Josephat and Bosco to a shot of whisky. We also shared some red dessert wine with them, brought to us by a porter today. Two things are wrong in this sentence : (1) dessert wine and (2) today... We had asked that a bottle of Namaqua Shiraz, which we knew was available in the local store, be delivered to us at Kitandara to celebrate our summit attempt. Instead, we received it a day later, and definitely not the dry red wine we had asked for. We tasted it, but despite it being not entirely unpalatable, and not as sweet as we expected, we didn't have more than a sip each. The guides however seemed to like it okay enough. So, it didn't go to waste.

Later, I sleep well knowing there's less than three hours to the park gate the next morning.

## Day 9: Nyabitaba to Nyakalengija (1646m)

*Time / distance / height-loss: 2-3hrs, 8.6km, 1006m*

A short hike this morning brought us back to the park gates where we started. Lots of praise and congratulations from the park staff and certificates to mark our achievement. It is an amazing experience to be standing 5km above sea level, and a privilege to have the opportunity to do so.

Doing so without the support of the porters (one of which, Amon, shepherded me on the non-technical parts of the trip), and the guides, would make this even more difficult than it is.

Sadly, they are exploited by many tour organisers. I discovered yesterday that they earn 10,000 Ugandan shillings – less than 3 USD per day… I also know that given what we are paying the tour company, the porters should earn a lot more than that! Even sadder is the fact that this exploitation is by the tour organisers. Guides, who put their lives at risk to protect us, don't fare much better, getting about 10 USD per day.

At 5000m I was walking and chewing on an energy bar... a quarter energy bar to be exact... I had to stop after a few steps to catch my breath... who would have thought the simple process of chewing could be that hard...

While peeling the shells of a boiled egg, I noticed that I was leaving black muddy finger marks on the white egg... then it went in my mouth without a further thought...

I also wondered if my mother's warnings about not washing my hands after I've been to the toilet will come true...

On the last morning we were all brought to near tears when we found out that Ronald, the assistant chef's brother had died the previous day. It didn't stop him from preparing our breakfast. And he would have carried on serving us if I didn't send him home...

We passed by the family home on our way to Kasese. Hundreds of people were gathering for the funeral. All expecting to be fed for taking the trouble to attend the funeral. A cow and several goats will be slaughtered to feed the masses. The burial party gets a goat of their own. As does the senior uncle of the departed...

Before our adventure, Mandy had never walked with crampons or held an ice axe, let alone climb a solid ice wall, and despite admitting to wanting to cry and/or be sick on a few occasions, and particularly on an exposed traverse, made it to the top and back.

After two-and-a-bit days of travelling from Kasese in Uganda via Entebbe and Nairobi (we spent a night in each), and the obligatory stop at the equator (where we took photos, watched the water run in different directions, and warded off merchants selling all kinds of curios), we arrived in Nanyuki to spend the night in a cheap 'hotel'.

Moses Njagi, my friend and guide on previous Mount Kenya trips, was to be our guide for this trip. Moses taught me a lot about Mount Kenya. He also taught me the names of plants and some of their peculiar uses, and about the spoor of elephant, buffalo, hyena, and their droppings. He would check how fresh the animal droppings were to gauge how close or far the animals may be from our position. Showed me how a hyena was following a young buffalo, possibly in the hope that the young won't survive. Moses passed away in 2018. I learnt a lot of from Moses which I hope to share with others.

We would meet up with Duncan, technical climbing guide, later.

Shortly after we arrived in Nanyuki, Moses set off to organise porters and cooks to support us during the trip. We saw him again around dinnertime, which was served in the large dining hall. Dinner was palatable, and no more needs to be said…

For those who don't know much about Mount Kenya, here are a few details about this majestic mountain. It is the second-highest mountain in Africa. Its twin summits are Batian (5,199m) and Nelion (5,188m) which can only be reached via a technical climb of minimum UIAA grade III difficulty. Most people who visit Mount Kenya summit Point Lenana (4,985m), the third highest peak, which can be reached by most walkers with a minimal amount of rock scrambling. Point Lenana is also known as the tourist summit.

Mount Kenya was created about three million years ago. Long before Adam arrived. It is a stratovolcano, estimated to have been about 7000m tall before the first glaciation period. In other words, it was higher than Kilimanjaro. Covered by a permanent ice cap for thousands of years, which eroded the peaks into the shapes as we know them today.

The name itself remains a bit of a mystery. One explanation is that the Kikuyu people living on its southern and western flanks had named it *Kirima Kĩrĩ Nyaga* (Mount Kirinyaga), which figuratively speaking means 'the mountain with white patches'. The Kamba (or Wakamba) people, southern neighbours of the Kikuyu translated Kirinyaga to *ki nyaa*. This was the name given to the German missionary Ludwig Kraph when he first sighted the mountain on 3 December 1849, a year after Mount Kilimanjaro was first sighted. He recorded the name as 'Kenya'. It became the name of the mountain and the country. The names of the three main peaks all commemorate Maasai chieftains. Batian after Mbatian, a Maasai medicine man. Nelion after Nelieng, brother of Mbatian, and Lenana after one of his sons. Sendeyo, another prominent peak is named after the second son of Mbatian. Other peaks have been named after European climbers like Shipton and Tilman, local personalities, and Jesus's disciples.

The mountain consists of multiple vegetation zones, with a distinct variation between Northern and Southern slopes between an altitude of about 2000 and 3000m. The drier northern slopes being mainly Savannah, while the wetter Southern side is covered in a montane forest and a bamboo zone. At about 3000m the zones converge and become an upper montane zone. This becomes an Ericaceous zone (heathland) at about 3500m, before turning into a typical Alpine zone at about 4000m. Giant lobelias and senecios, both endemic to Mount Kenya, grow in the heathland zone. Elephants, Buffalo, Hyrax, Antelope, Hyena and Leopards, and the occasional Lion all roam its slopes.

Being situated almost on the equator (about sixteen-and-a-half kilometres south of the equator), Mount Kenya enjoys a constant twelve hours of daylight. Sunrise is at about 0630 and sunset is at about 1830. The shortest and longest day differs by one minute.

## FIRST ASCENT OF MOUNT KENYA

According to Kikuyu belief God (*Ngai* or *Mwene Ngaya*) lived on the mountain. *Gĩkũyũ* – the father of the tribe would meet here with *Ngai*, which, in Kikuyu folklore makes Gĩkũyũ the first person to have climbed Mount Kenya.

However, in Alpine folklore this honour belongs to Sir Halford John Mackinder who set out on 28 July 1899 from what we today know as Nairobi, joined by six Europeans, sixty-six Swahilis, two Maasai guides, and ninety-six Kikuyu, heading for Mount Kenya. Along the way some Kikuyu Porters tried to desert with women from the villages and others stole from the villagers, which made local chiefs hostile towards the expedition.

They reached their base camp on 18 August, but unable to find food, and having had two of their party killed by locals they had to send for help. While one of the party members, Saunders, went for help in Naivashu, Mackinder pushed on and established a camp at 3,142m in the Höhnel Valley.

On 30 August he made his first attempt on the summit but had to retreat 100m below the summit of Nelion due to nightfall. Mackinder made another attempt after Saunders returned with the relief party. This time Mackinder, Ollier and Brocherel succeeded, reaching the summit of Batian on 13 September 1899 via the Diamond Glacier.

Nelion, had to wait almost thirty years, until on 6 January 1929 Percy Wyn-Harris and Eric Shipton reached its summit.

## THE MOUNT KENYA CLIMB

### Day 1: Sirimon Gate to Judmaier's (Old Moses) camp (3300m)

*Time / distance / height-gain: 3-3.5 hrs, 9km, 650m*

Moses and the cook left early this morning with a few thousand Kenyan shillings to stock up on supplies. Our pile of equipment and food started growing where we were waiting for them to return. Sometime late morning, a couple of clapped-out but perfectly serviceable Land Rovers arrived and started loading our collection of baggage. Soon we were on our way to the Sirimon gate (2650m), the North westerly entrance to Mount Kenya National park, where I filled in reams of forms and paid park and camp fees. I think that the Sirimon to Chogoria crossing provides some of the best all-round views of the mountains. It's also a much gentler start than some of the other starting points, giving you a chance to ease into the trek and in the process acclimatise better (although I have seen a party suffering from altitude sickness even at Old Moses camp), before picking up pace on day three and four, when the real challenges start.

After tea and lunch, and me having a moan at Moses for not having enough porters, and him disappearing to organise more people, we started walking to reach our first overnight camp, Old Moses, just as it started raining (this is meant to be the 'dry season', by the way…).

Note: I feel strongly about the porters not carrying more than a reasonable load. Many guides and guiding companies will overload the porters to save costs and put more profit in their own pockets. This, in my opinion, is unethical and being done at the cost of the long-term health of these amazing people who carry our clothes, tents, food and other supplies up and down the mountains, with hardly a moan. It is one of the key reasons I started my own company arranging trips to Africa's highest mountains, so that I can – in a small way – try and make a difference by providing guiding services that do not exploit the locals, pay them a living wage, and put as much money as possible back into the local community.

## Day 2: Old Moses camp to Shipton's Camp (4236m)

*Time / distance / height-gain: 6-7 hrs, 17km, 936m*

We started our walk in the rain, managed to get our raincoats off for half an hour and then spent the next four plus hours in more freezing rain… Neither Mandy (who re-joined André and I in Nanyuki) nor I were adequately dressed for this unexpected weather. I had a t-shirt, a thin jumper, and my rain jacket on. Mandy only had a thin insulated weatherproof jacket on. Both of us arrived at Shipton's Camp in a half-frozen state, where we had hoped to be able to warm up at the fire… Except, there was no fire, and to have a fire you have to bring your own charcoal, so we found out, somewhat belatedly. Our porters and thus our warm clothes would take another two hours to get here… Mandy, if it was possible, was even more frozen than I was, and in a semi-hypothermic state. I was cold but felt I could get through this. I made her put my thin jumper on under her jacket and gave her my socks and rain pants for added warmth. Mahendra, a German we met at Old Moses that day before, filled his water bottle with hot water, and gave it to Mandy to help her warm up. With her feet on the hot water bottle, and me sitting behind her back, we managed to warm her a few degrees. Mountain people looking after each other…

Great was our joy and relief when our clothes finally arrived. To my dismay I discovered that my clothes had wet patches. But wet patches or not, they would still make me a hundred times warmer than what I was. On they went. A couple of hot brews later we crawled into our sleeping bags for more warmth, staying there until dinner was served. Still not completely rewarmed. But at least out of the danger zone. My back, which I hurt when I picked up my bag at Kasese, and probably not helped by today's cold, had become extremely uncomfortable. I couldn't sit comfortably in any position, and the Ibuprofen only helped for a few hours at a time.

## Day 3: Shipton's camp

After dinner on Tuesday evening I went outside, and there was a dazzling display of stars, lifting spirits and hope for clear weather the next day. Alas, when I got up, it was clear that this was not to be. The morning started with the peaks wrapped in thick layers of clouds.

We had agreed with Moses to go to Point Lenana at nine in the morning, but with the clouds as low as they were and visibility zero, we delayed. Eventually at about ten, Moses set off with André and Mandy in tow. I had been to Point Lenana before, and given that my pack was still sopping wet, I decided to stay behind to try and dry it for the next day's intended climb (and start writing that book everyone has been mentioning…).

## Abandoning the climb

Wednesday about 14.00… It has rained some more; the cloud cover has thickened, and a strong wind is blowing. Duncan and I have a chat, and we agree that a) this being the dry season the rain is likely to last for possibly another two days (three to four days is typical for wet spells during the dry season), and b) of greater concern, the combination of mist / rain plus strong winds will result in ice crystals forming on the rock – and in particular on the route that we should be following the next day, which could stay in place for a day or two. We agree to call off the climb and retreat from the mountain, which would then enable us to rearrange the Kilimanjaro timetable and come back afterwards to climb Batian.

Despite the lateness of the afternoon and knowing that if we leave now it would mean walking in the dark for part of the way, I'm freezing and decide that a couple of hours of headlamp walking with a warm hut waiting at the other end with 1) fireplace 2) warm shower 3) cold beer, beats sitting and shivering in our current hut.

Duncan looks equally keen to get off the mountain, so we decide to leave at 4pm on what's supposed to be a six-to-seven-hour walk. André is not keen on walking in the dark and prefers to spend the night. Mandy wants to come along but decides that she'll slow us up and decides to stay.

So, now should I go on my own? Or stay? I decided that I've shivered enough for one day/week/month… The walk in the dark is a minor trade-off by comparison. We decide to set off. Duncan and I with two porters Simon and Boneface. And a bag of maize meal and some veg to make a stew to eat with the ugali (putu for my South African friends).

## Shipton's camp to Meru Mount Kenya bandas

*Time / distance / height-gain/loss: 6-7 hrs, 19.8km, +490m / -1741m*

We're at the 'roadhead' at 8pm, four hours after we set off and now less than forty-five mins away from the bandas. The path is very wet and slippery, and we're forced to go slower.

Hall's Tarn with Mount Kenya in the background

As we approach the river Duncan starts hitting his walking sticks together to warn away stray buffalo and elephant bulls who are known to roam this area. We don't come across any (I was wondering which of the gang I would have to outrun, if we were chased...) and not long after, at about 9.30pm we arrive at the bandas, greeted by the shiny eyes of a herd of buffalo grazing in front of the bandas (huts) and Jarvin the hut keeper and his helper Washington. A few minutes later the fire is on the go, the shower is ready, and the beers are on their way...

Footnote: Boneface is pronounced bonnie face, and not bone face which may be an obvious name for the young man, given his high cheekbones... Boneface is apparently a top-class runner. He and Simon are close friends. Simon is probably a real lady-killer. Tall and well-built he stands out among his peers. He's training under Duncan to be a guide and hopes to go to Germany for further climbing training. Duncan I've known for some time and consider him a friend, despite the client/guide relationship while we're on the mountain. Solid and dependable, we see things in a similar way making for a great mountaineering partnership.

## Day 4: Retreating. Back to Nairobi

The rest of the gang arrived shortly after breakfast. I paid the porters for the full trip, despite our cutting it short. I called each one individually, thanked them, paid them their salary, and added a tip. The smiles on their faces suggested that the money was appreciated. I was left wishing I was able to double the amount. Then we left in the Land Rovers that arrived while I was paying the people that put us on the mountain.

Meru Bandas the morning after I retreated

While licking our wounds, I decided I had to get rid of the back pain, which I had guessed was caused by a trapped nerve. I got myself flat on the stone floor in the bedroom and managed to manoeuvre myself into a sort of yoga pose. With one leg straightened out and the knee of the other leg pulled up to my chin, I stretched and suddenly felt something snap – like a rubber band, and with that came complete relief. My back, which had been worrying me for days, was completely stress and pain free.

While we were walking in the dark yesterday evening, Boneface slipped and I caught him, stopping him from falling. It struck me that at that moment the roles of client, guide, porter no longer existed. Tomorrow when I pay them, the roles will come back into play, but right then we were just four men making our way off a mountain. Class, colour, culture, any differences we may have, disappearing into the mists that surrounded us...

After a couple of days recovering in Nairobi, including a long visit to the lovely Thorn Tree Café in the Stanley hotel, where I could sort out pics and make notes, it was time to travel to Tanzania. To the snows of Kilimanjaro. The highest peak in Africa. The highest free-standing mountain in the world. The mountain that rises nearly five vertical kilometres above the surrounding plateau…

Mandy has gone off somewhere down the East coast of Kenya towards Zanzibar, from where she may eventually travel onwards to South Africa. Or not. Depending on which way the wind blows.

So, it's going to be André and me on this climb with our support team consisting of two guides, a cook, and his assistant, and eight porters.

My friend Ronaldo, who was meant to have organised the trip, was still somewhere on the mountain supporting a large group, and we had to make do with his office assistant to organise our support crew. This would lead to a few problems along the way, including the guides and porters not having been adequately informed of our intentions to ascend via the Western Breach, and the assistant, probably trying to save his boss a few Tanzanian shillings, hiring tents that were well past their use by date, and totally inadequate for the cold and wind we encountered on the mountain…

If you've never heard of Kilimanjaro, then I have a few things I can tell you about this majestic lady.

Not only is Kilimanjaro the highest mountain in Africa and the highest free-standing peak in the world, it is also the fourth highest peak in terms of prominence – i.e., the minimum height that has to be ascended to reach its summit. It is also the highest volcano outside South America. Like Mount Kenya it is stratospheric in origin. (A stratospheric volcano consists of multiple layers [strata] caused by multiple eruptions. It is conical in shape with a typically steep profile and summit crater, which may have collapsed forming a 'caldera'.)

Kilimanjaro is made up of three distinct volcanic cones: Kibo – classified as dormant, and Mawenzi (5,149m) and Shira (4,005m), both classed as extinct. Uhuru Peak, the highest peak on Kilimanjaro, was known as Kaiser-Wilhelm-Spitze until 1964 when Tanzania was formed. It was renamed Uhuru Peak which means 'freedom peak' in Kiswahili.

## FIRST ASCENT OF MOUNT KILIMANJARO

After several unsuccessful attempts, including one expedition, where Meyer and his climbing partner were taken hostage and ransomed by hostile local tribesmen, Hans Meyer, Ludwig Purtscheller (an Austrian mountaineer) and Yohani Kinyala Lauwo, (a Chagga villager who guided the expedition) made it to the top of Uhuru Peak on 6 October 1889.

More than hundred-and-twenty-five years later, André and I were on our way to make our own first ascent of the magnificent Kilimanjaro. Via the seldom travelled Western Breach route.

## THE KILIMANJARO CLIMB

## Day 1: Umbwe Gate to Umbwe Cave Camp (2850m)

*Time / distance / height-gain: 5-7 hrs, 10.5km, 1250m*

I woke up this morning realising that we're about to climb a big mountain. While she may not offer many technical challenges, she more than makes up for it in height… by the time we summit, we'll have climbed nearly four-and-a-half vertical kilometres. which feels like a long, long way right now…

While having a last cup of tea and waiting for the transport to arrive to take us to Umbwe Gate (1600m) in Kilimanjaro National Park, a hundred other thoughts are going through my head. Are we adequately prepared? Are we fit enough? Will the weather be kind to us? Etc, etc, etc… Then our transport – a minibus for us and the guides, and a small bus for the porters and our equipment arrive. As soon as they're packed, we set off for the Umbwe gate. All thoughts of 'are we this?', 'are we that?', instantly dispelled and the focus shifts to the challenge ahead.

Ronaldo has arranged two highly experienced guides in the persons of Willy and Gideon. Willy will turn out to be the more conservative of the two and try his best to discourage us from climbing the Western Breach route we had set out to do. Gideon appeared to be much happier to accommodate us. Either way before we got to the summit, we still had a fair amount of negotiation to do to get the crew on board.

At one stage there was even talk about us carrying some of our own gear and travelling with a skeleton crew – the remainder travelling via the more touristy route and meeting us on our descent. All this was settled when we paid the extra fee for the 'extra risk' that they would be exposed to in ascending the mountain via the Western Breach. Whether it was lack of communication from our chief 'organiser', or perhaps he simply did not mention it in order to get the crew signed up and then leaving it up to us to negotiate we'll never know.

The drive to Umbwe gate takes us through coffee plantations, and private smallholdings. As you enter the park, the scenery changes. While the porters were sorting and weighing kit, with the ever-present Colobus monkeys looking on, we were completing paperwork and providing proof that payment for permits and camp fees had been made. Then, after a pre-packed picnic lunch, and stocking up with bottles of water, we set off… our climb to the summit of Kilimanjaro is under way.

The first part of the walk is on a vehicle track, which soon becomes a single track-maintained footpath. The jungle is thick with vine-covered trees reaching up to the heavens above. Here and there the sun creeps through the mist, creating a fascinating spectacle.

It does not take long for me to fall under the spell of this majestic mountain, and by the time we reach Umbwe Camp, I know that I should have been here long ago.

## Day 2: Umbwe Cave camp to Barranco Camp (3900m)

*Time / distance / height-gain: 4-6 hrs, 6.5km, 1050m*

The campsite, despite it not being on the flattest part of the mountain, turns out to be a superb site. The nearly full moon cast a light glow over our tents, which consist of mine and André's tents, a mess, and a toilet tent, plus the cook's tent, and the porters' accommodation. It's going to take a crew of twelve people to put the two of us on top of the mountain.

During the night I hear Colobus Monkeys playing in the trees above, sometimes right above us. And when I wake in the morning, it's to the sound of birdsong. A perfect start to what will turn out to be a gloriously sunny day for us, well above the clouds that are covering the lowlands.

After breakfast, we are introduced to the crew. Gideon is the chief guide, Willy the second-in-command. Ally is the chef and Mgaya is his assistant and our ever-attentive 'waiter'. Then there's Edwin who has the unenviable task of cleaning the portable toilets every morning and carrying them (empty) to the next campsite (I dubbed him the 'chemical engineer'), plus another seven porters who will be carrying our personal equipment, tents, mattresses, tables, chairs, food, and water, as well as their own equipment. In bags, on top of their heads through four-thousand vertical metres and fifty kilometres, and always with a smile on their faces. After the introductions we were treated to some singing – including a modified version of 'Jambo bwana' (think Lion King) …

Then we set off for day two's trek. We're still in the forest zone. Surrounded by grand old yellow trees, olive trees, huge tree ferns and a host of other giant trees with vines reminiscent of Tarzan films. While walking through the beautiful rainforest, I say to André that I'm beginning to think we should have come here a long time ago…

Our first break, for snacks, is at about 3600m. We've now entered the heather zone, with the vegetation a lot sparser. Old man's beard is draped around the trees, and through a gap in the trees I get my first glimpse of the peak ahead.

We're now higher than the Drakensberg where we both learnt our mountain skills, with another two-hundred vertical metres to our campsite.

Barranco Camp at the head of the Barranco Valley looks like a tent village. This campsite being at a junction of three main routes (Machame, Lemosho and Shira), you end up with a few hundred people here on any trekking day. We estimate that there may be as many as five-hundred people camping at the site.

Fortunately, our camp is pitched somewhat away from the rest, with our own private toilet tent. Giving us some privacy. I dub our camp Snob Hill. Gratefully.

While having lunch I saw a large bird gliding towards the mess tent. Realised that it was a Bearded Vulture (now called Bartgeier in German, which is much nicer than the original misnomer 'lammergeier'). I got super excited, ran outside, and called André to come and watch this magnificent creature gliding past, less than ten metres away and almost directly above us. Passing so close that I could clearly see the beard that gave rise to its common English name, 'Bearded Vulture'. It continued down along the spur of the valley we were camping on. At the bottom of the spur the wing tips turned up, braking and then it turned 180° and continued up the left bank of the adjacent spur, doing another 180° turn at the apex before gliding down the right bank, flying so low, and being so well camouflaged, that had we not been able to see its shadow on the shrubs and plants below, we would not have known it was there. One more turn took it up the next spur and then it was gone…

Barranco Camp with Kibo in cloud

## Day 3: Barranco Camp to Lava Tower Camp (4642m)

*Time / distance / height-gain: 4–6 hrs, 14km, 742m*

The day starts with breakfast… and then we're off with our day packs while the crew starts packing up the camp.

Willy keeps reminding us to walk 'pole-pole' (slowly-slowly). After nearly three weeks of running around at altitude, we're both acclimatised and comfortable walking at a faster than 'pole-pole' pace.

At our lunch stop I duck behind the nearest rock to have a pee and discover a total mess. Little piles of toilet paper and excrement everywhere. While I can understand people's need for toilet breaks in the wild, I fail to understand why they can't take their waste with them. Or, at the very least, the paper they use which they can stuff in a plastic bag and burn, or dispose of in the chemical toilet, at the next camp. I feel disgusted and annoyed with my fellow human beings for their lack of respect for nature and their fellow trekkers.

When we reach the Lava Tower Camp, the crew is busy setting up camp. Once settled in our tents, we decide to scale the tower. Willy and Suleimon, one of the porters, join us. Suleimon is one of the younger porters in the crew. He looked ever so eager when I asked if any of them wanted to join us. He's a bright and friendly young man who wants to become a guide. He is the only Muslim in the group, and soon after we had set up camp this afternoon, he took his sleeping mat and went to do his prayers on a rock outcrop just above us. A few of those prayers, I'd like to think, were for our safe passage.

A balmy sunny afternoon ended with a very rapid temperature drop to about 4 or 5°C. Both André and I donned long johns and added extra layers before sitting down at the dinner table.

A little drop of Johnny Walker raised the inner temperature and the warm soup and chapatis did the rest. Shortly after dinner I crawl into my sleeping bag with a hot water bottle at my feet. (The hot water bottle serves a double purpose. The porters fetch water from uncertain sources. Boiling it is the only way to ensure that it's not full of harmful bacteria. By pouring it into your water bottles the night before, it's cold when you drink it the next day, and it adds a few degrees of warmth to the sleeping bag.)

Somewhere around midnight I wake and after debating with myself whether I should use the pee bottle or not decided to venture out into the cold to look at the stars. With the moon nearly full the mountain looks stunningly beautiful and I once again ask myself why I haven't made this trip before…

## Day 4: Lava Tower Camp to Arrow Glacier Camp (4803m)

*Time / distance / height-gain: 1.5 – 2 hrs, 5km, 161m*

Our walk today is a super short one. Height gained only hundred-and-sixty-one metres. Nothing. Yes, tell my lungs that… they think differently. Last night's sleep was definitely more difficult than the previous night's sleep. Comparable perhaps to our high camp on Mount Stanley. Struggling to breathe, constantly waking. Happy when the sun comes out and you can get up… even if you did not get enough sleep.

Because we have a very short walk today, we sleep much later. Somehow, as the sun comes up and it gets warmer, I find I sleep a bit better. Breakfast is the normal feast.

Then, a short one-and-a-half hour's walking brings us to the Arrow Glacier Camp. A small shelf devoid of vegetation. We're in the Highland desert zone. Very little rain falls here. About two-hundred millimetres per year. A teacup full. You're surrounded by stones. From tiny pebbles not much bigger than a grain of sand, to stones the size of a multi-storey house. Lots of lava rock lying about. Weighing next to nothing. Our tents are pitched among this strangely fascinating collection of rubble.

Porters making their way up from Lava Tower Camp

We spend the afternoon doing as little as possible. Getting as much rest as possible in preparation for tomorrow's final push to the crater. Above us the Western breach is clearly visible.

According to Gideon, our camp site was still covered in a foot-thick layer of ice as little as fifteen years ago. Now the only remaining glaciers are patches clinging doggedly to the crevices of the ridge.

It was the melting of these ice patches which caused a rockslide in 2005, killing three people on the route to the Western breach. Apparently not far above from where we are camping. The route was closed for a few years while an investigation was conducted and eventually reopened after a safer and more protected passage was proposed.

Then in 2015 another climber was killed when a large rock came loose, giving the route a reputation for being dangerous. Which it is. But every route on Kilimanjaro has the potential for rockfall, and lives have been claimed on other routes too, although not three at the same time. Or even if they had, they did not receive the media coverage the 2005 incident did.

So, why are we following a route that is understood to be more dangerous than the other routes? Many reasons for me: We're not surrounded by a circus of tourists; the climb is a grade 2 or 3 scramble, making it feel more like a serious climb than a walk to the top; we summited in daytime, had the summit and the crater to ourselves; explored the ash pit; slept in the crater. Okay, you're not convinced. I understand. So, how about I just say we climbed the Western breach route because it's there…

For what it's worth. The fact that most operators will advise clients not to do the Western breach, means that while the campsite at Barranco may have had as many as five-hundred people camping, last night at Lava Tower camp, and again tonight André and I together with our team are the only people at our campsite. And what magnificent campsites both have been.

## Day 5: Arrow Glacier camp to Reusch Crater camp (5734m)

*Time / distance / height-gain: 7-8 hrs, 2km, 940m*

It's Thursday morning, the day we will reach the top of Kilimanjaro.

05.00: Gideon or Willy taps on the tent and says morning. I'm awake. When I respond he moves on to André's tent and does the same. On previous days we didn't move from our warm sleeping bags until the sun reached our camp. Somewhere between 08.00 and 08.30. And didn't start walking until after 10.00 the day before. Today however the cold that we avoided on previous days is our friend.

The Western Breach Route follows a line through the western rock barrier below Uhuru Peak. This rock barrier is a precariously stacked pile of blocks of various sizes piled on top of each other forming tall pillars, 'glued' together with a layer of ice. Stacked side by side they resemble organ pipes, but without the smoothness.

At night-time the temperature drops, and the ice expands, pushing the blocks apart a little fraction at a time. Next day as the outer layer of ice turns into water it flows down and fills the gap caused by the expansion. Next night this water freezes and expands, repeating the action of pushing the blocks apart. So, at the same time as the ice is trying its best to hold the pile of blocks together, it is also trying its best to push them apart. While it's cold, the rock pile is in a fairly stable state. But as the sun warms the rocks, those that have been pushed apart to the point where they are overbalancing, are released and tumble down.

This has resulted in an area of a few hundred metres that has been demarcated as a 'rockfall corridor', i.e., where the greatest incidence of falling rocks occur. We call it a rockfall zone. In any other language it will be called a danger zone. It is this rockfall corridor that you must cross early morning, while the ice is holding the rocks together, to reduce the risk of rock being hurled at you.

Despite the sign that informs that you must leave before 05.30, at about 06.15 Gideon, Willy, André, and I set off on the path that leads up and through the Western Breach. The porters are in the process of breaking camp as we depart. They'll be on our heels soon enough and overtaking us before too long. The wind is screaming at us as we leave and within a few hundred metres my fingers are frozen. The kind of frozen that's so sore that you want to bite your fingertips off. It doesn't take long for my toes to reach the same stage. Despite the intense cold I feel mentally sharp and relaxed.

Constantly on the alert for any sounds of rock falling. Constantly on the lookout for large boulders that I might be able to dive behind if a rock tries to attack me. Constantly keeping an eye on my three companions – knowing where they are in relation to me. Our combined alertness can make the difference between being hit or missed if there is a rockfall. Inwardly, quietly sighing, and relaxing as we reach the 'stone train', a vertical rib of rock, providing cover and protection from potential rockfall above.

Past the danger point, heading up towards the breach

We stop for a water break while our porters with loads of 20kg balanced on their heads, icicles formed on their upper lips stream past.

Higher up, we stop again for a cup of thick black sugary coffee and some biscuits that Willy digs out of his bag. I squirt an energy gel into my mouth and have a few bites of energy bar. Not too much, as the chewing leaves me breathless. (Almost every movement at this altitude leaves you breathless. Turning in your sleeping bag. Pulling your boots on. Tying your shoelaces. Unzipping the tent. Going to the toilet. Even breathing seems to leave you breathless!)

Then we're off again. Uhuru Peak looming above us and getting nearer until finally, we break through the last rock band and a short diagonal walk later, we're in the crater. Four-and-a-quarter hours after we started. High-fives, handshakes, and hugs are exchanged. To our left we have a glacier that looks like a giant iceberg – the remainder of the Furtwängler Glacier. On our right, the crater rim on which Uhuru Peak sits. In front of us one giant sandpit that we have to cross to get to our campsite.

In the Reusch Crater – the dwindling Northern Icefields visible on the left

Note: most route descriptions tell you that it will take you about seven to eight hours to cover the two kilometres (plus nine-hundred vertical metres). André and I must have been in a hurry, we covered this distance in four-and-a-quarter hours.

## Thursday 11.00. To the summit.

After finding some ibuprofen in my bag to doctor one of our porters who is complaining of a serious headache (probably suffering from altitude sickness), Gideon, André and I set off for the summit. We'd already gained about eight-hundred-and-fifty vertical metres today and this last nearly one hundred and fifty metres turns out to be extra, extra tough going. André comments when we get to the top of the ridge connected to the summit that a winch would have been useful…

At 11.59 we reach the signboard that tells you that you have reached the top of Africa. Nothing special about it. Just another mountain top. And yet… as I look around me at the scenery, the Reusch Crater to my left with the impressive ash pit in the middle of it, Mawenzi below and in front of me, the Southern ice fields to my right, a clear blue sky above, and a sign behind me that says you've made it, I wonder, with a little more emotion than I'd care to admit, why I waited so long to climb Kilimanjaro.

On top of the world

## The Reusch crater

The Reusch crater, for those interested in the history, is named after a German missionary who worked in the Kilimanjaro area. He was the first climber to spot the crater, when he made his first ascent in 1926 (other climbers ascending via different routes). In 1954, the Tanzanian (Tanganyikan) government named the crater after Gustav Otto Richard Reusch when he reached the summit for the twenty-fifth time. He went on to attempt the climb to the summit another forty times. Reusch was the first to spot a carcass of a frozen leopard near the summit. The photos that he took of the frozen leopard, was apparently the inspiration for Hemingway to write the 'The Snows of Kilimanjaro'.

## Day 6: The Ash pit and descent to Mweka Gate (1653m)

*Time / distance / height-loss: 7-8 hrs, 20km, 4147m*

As if sleeping in the crater at an altitude of about 5734m wasn't going to be difficult enough, with temperatures in the minus teens, we were battered by a wind that, at times, threatened to rip the tent from the ground. Making our night even more memorable, was the fact that the penny-saving 'organiser' who had rented the tents for our use, had hired the cheapest possible models with the most broken parts and holes for extra ventilation. Zips sometimes closed. Sometimes they didn't. Other times they'd pull apart and leave gaps. Guides and porters were constantly trying to fix one zip or another. Pin-sized holes in the tent wall allowed the wind to whistle through and torment. At lower altitudes it was easy to tolerate and forget. But at 5800m this became a constant source of discomfort.

But that was only a minor inconvenience when compared with our lack of ability to breathe… Sleeping at this altitude is most definitely not the easiest thing I've ever done. Several times during the night, I woke – unable to breathe. Feeling like someone is standing on my chest and stopping me from being able to breathe properly. Desperately trying to get a decent amount of oxygen into my lungs I'd keep breathing in, with every breath feeling shallower than the previous one. Eventually, a single deep breath slips through, and for a while I feel a bit calmer. After a while I'd drift off. Exhausted from the battle to breathe. Then it starts all over again. Someone jumps on my chest, and I start the battle for that one life-giving breath all over again. It's at this point that you begin to understand why mountaineers use supplementary oxygen when sleeping at altitude.

André and I were chatting to friends a couple of years after the trip, about the experience of sleeping at this altitude. He said that he did not sleep at all. He was too scared he would not wake up again if he went to sleep... I can understand that.

Fortunately, the sun reached the crater much earlier than the western side we had ascended and by seven we were both out of our tents and ready to go. We told Ally to keep breakfast simple. Coffee and scrambled eggs. Gas cookers do not operate efficiently at high altitude... and apart from the two of us, he had thirteen other people to feed... Mgaya, porter, cook's helper, waiter, and chief hugger whenever we arrived at a new destination, arrived with our morning flask of coffee... most apologetically announcing that the milk was finished. Thick. Black. And full of sediment, possibly thanks to a much lower boiling point (we estimated boiling point would have been somewhere around 80°C at this altitude).

Gideon, meanwhile, in addition to the chest infection he developed (I'd had him on antibiotics for two days by this time), had now also developed symptoms of altitude sickness: headache, nausea, upset stomach. We told him to pack up and get off the mountain as soon as possible and wait for us at Barafu camp about a thousand metres lower.

So now, with a porter who in addition to his headache had now also developed a sore leg, a guide whose chest infection wasn't going to improve at altitude and with André starting to lose his voice, and beginning to show the same symptoms as Gideon, we decided that if we go well on our descent to Millennium Camp, that we'd go all the way to the gate. A trip that would normally take two days.

## The Ash pit

Shortly after 7.30 am, André, Willy and I set off for the Ash Pit. Pole, pole, one last time, as we slowly made our way up the crater wall. As we topped the crater rim, we were hit by a wind of jet speed proportion that tried its utmost to blow us back to where we had come from. With the wind came a strong smell of sulphur. Like the smell of rotten eggs. Nauseating. Dangerous. Fortunately, we were on a level patch and could speed away from the sulphurous gas relatively quickly. Safely away from the gas, we had time to start enjoying this amazing left-over from a volcanic eruption that happened more than two-hundred-thousand years ago.

The Ash Pit

The inner core is a near perfect concentric funnel, surrounded by a level valance containing a mixture of lava rock, sulphur, volcanic sand, sedimentary rocks, etc... some of it looking like it had been shot from a cannon, others as if it had been neatly arranged in long arching rows.

Due to the strong wind which must have pushed the temperature into the minus twenties or below we didn't go all the way to the inner core, skirting the edge of the valance before making our way out of the crater and onto its rim, then circumnavigating it, while making our way towards Stella Point, from where we would start our descent.

## Descent to Millennium Camp

At two minutes past ten we stood at Stella Point. Apparently, the 'normal' descent from here to Barafu Camp takes about two to three hours. We did it in fifty-nine minutes. Twenty minutes after arriving here we left and made our way to Millennium Camp (pronounced 'Mirrennium Camp' by the locals) where the crew were preparing lunch.

While eating, I said to André, I'd love to get rid of my thermal bottom-layer. That however would have meant having to remove boots, trousers, socks. And with thought came the realisation that every stitch of clothing I'm wearing has been on my body for about thirty-six hours... in the end I left the thermals (and the rest) on and didn't take anything off until I was safely in my hotel room where I could safely remove all the layers and dump them in a bin-bag to be taken directly to a washing machine.

While the porters and guides were having lunch André and I managed a quick but very welcome nap. All too soon a much-improved Gideon was calling us for the next leg of our descent – a muscle jarring final sixteen kilometres and more than 2000 vertical metres. A little over two and a half hours later we arrived at Mweka Gate, to hugs and cheers from our porters and porters from other parties we had passed on our way down.

The only thing left to do for us was to sign out, get our certificates, pack the van, and drive to the nearest place where we could treat ourselves and our porters to a cold drink and present them with a tip to say thanks for making it possible for us to have reached the top of Africa.

The Kilimanjaro team – celebrating with a beer

The quest having been to complete all three of Africa's highest peaks, means this challenge is not over. I had the time and opportunity to return to Kenya and complete the climb, but André had duties to perform back at home, and since this challenge was started with André, I intend finishing it with André. One day.

The adventure started for me when I went to Tenerife to climb Mount Teide. The one that Spanish bureaucracy denied me and will have to wait until later to complete. From there I went to the Atlas Mountains in Morocco and despite a freezing wind that drove a lot of people off the mountain, Hassan and I summited. Ethiopia was my next stop. Ras Dejen, the highest peak in the Simien Mountains turned out to be a completely different experience to what I had expected. From there I joined with André, and for part of the way with Mandy, to climb Mount Stanley, Mount Kenya, and Mount Kilimanjaro.

Besides experiencing the diversity of the mountains – the snow-covered Atlas overlooking the scorched earth of the Sahara, the bird-rich and dramatic Simien mountains, the lush and green Rwenzori, Mount Kenya where only a glimpse of the peak was seen thanks to unseasonal bad weather, and finally on to Mount Kilimanjaro – the doyen of African mountains with its terrain ranging from enchanting rainforest to the desert-like crater adorned with icebergs below its summit, there was the equally diverse human experience. I'll mention just a few…

Let me start with Mohamed. Young teacher in Northern Morocco who cannot get a teaching job. Great company and knowledgeable about his local area. Hassan who lives in the Atlas Mountains in Morocco. Friend and guide on multiple trips – a Berber who invited me into his house for dinner – a rare honour – and whose text messages I have to decipher phonetically (e.g., 'Hallo mfrin ioki' – which means "hello my friend, are you okay?"). Abera, steady, reliable – based in Debark, his experience ranging far beyond his native Simien mountains. Hosseini, the 74-year-old scout who was my shadow in the Simiens, and who greeted me like a brother when I said goodbye. Yrga the cook, who was ex-military and had seen service in Sudan as well as Eritrea – a gentle soul who prepared great dishes for me and the team. Josephat and Bosco who guided us to the top of Mount Stanley – technically the most difficult peak we ascended, involving ice climbing and a glacier crossing. At altitude. Happy the cook, who always had something encouraging and friendly to say. Moses, my partner, and guide on previous excursions on Mount Kenya – now sadly departed off this world. Duncan, my friend and possibly one of the most efficient guides I've met on the African continent. Gideon and Willy who guided us to the top of Kilimanjaro, where our greatest challenge was the altitude. Suleimon, the young Muslim who said his prayers diligently. Mgaya the hugger who would welcome us at each camp with a hug.

All people of Africa. Different. And yet the same. From 'darkest Africa' they may well be, but the blood that flows through their veins is a pure warm African red. Just like mine!

Was there one memory that defined this trip? For example, was getting to the top of Mount Stanley – the technically more difficult peak, more satisfying than reaching the much higher Mount Kilimanjaro – the top of Africa? Was the trip in the Rwenzori with its lush and green more interesting than Mount Kenya where elephants, leopards, and buffalo roam freely? Each of these are firmly etched into my brain. Each with special memories of their own.

But the memory that will last longest are the people who joined us on this incredible journey. And that's not just the guides who lead us safely, or the porters who happily bounced along with loads of twenty or more kilograms on or suspended from their heads, nor the chefs that kept our stomachs happy, the hosts at the various places we stayed along the way, or my climbing partners on Mount Stanley, Mount Kenya, and

Kilimanjaro. It was the people that were supporting me with their love, care, encouragement: friends – some of whom I've known since pre-school days; the cousins that I've known forever; my children – one of whom constantly worries that I might be abducted by a stray terrorist somewhere; climbing and trekking partners on many adventures; an ex-wife who continued to support me in my love of adventure; my girlfriend who was lighting a candle for us on the very day that we were flying down the slopes of Kilimanjaro. Those who sent private messages of encouragement, support, and love. You made this trip memorable! Thank you!

From that first moment of standing on top of the Drakensberg escarpment, to the very moment that I stood on top of Kilimanjaro, I have been utterly and hopelessly in love with mountains. Over the years I have learnt to respect the moods of mountains. I understood when they were angry, and I had to tread with care as the sky above changed to dark angry greys and streaks of lightning reached from the clouds to the earth while thunder turned my world into an amphitheatre of sound. I also knew when it was safe to skip along with carefree abandon as the sun bounced off every tip of grass or glistened in each patch of water. I was accompanied by friends while birds circled and tumbled and glided and watched me as I made my way. I've been surprised by the many animals appearing as if from nowhere on their slopes. I've watched the mountains don a coat of flowers in spring, as new life emerges from the ice-cold earth, and I've watched them put on an autumn coat, adorned with colours that even the most skilful painter can't mix together. I've rested in the shade of the trees along their flanks and been refreshed in the rivers that flow from their slopes. Perhaps most importantly, I've revelled in the bonding and the camaraderie, and the love and the support of the people that I've been fortunate enough to share this love affair with. Mountain people. And there was one particular moment on Mount Kenya that epitomised this bond for me. A moment I captured in a post to the WhatsApp group I started, to keep family and friends updated with our progress:

> *While we were walking in the dark yesterday evening, Boneface slipped and I caught him, stopping him from falling. It struck me that at that moment the roles of client, guide, porter no longer existed. Tomorrow when I pay them, they'll come back into play, but right then we were just four people making our way off a mountain. Class, colour, culture, any differences we may have, disappearing into the mists that surrounded us...*

During the course of our adventure I kept friends and family up to date with our progress. I never realised how important support from friends and family can be when you are on an expedition... To put it simply, they walked with me every step of the way.

To remind them of this little adventure, I've appended the original transcript of the original chat. (The only edits to this chat were to remove system messages, e.g., Group icon changed, so-and-so was added; so-and-so left the group, etc. Otherwise, this is uncut; typos and all.)

---

### 25 July 2016

---

You [**HARRY**] created group "3 Peaks African Adventure"

**HARRY:** Hi all. A few of you asked that I let you know how we get on with climbing Africa's Big Three Peaks... flying out tomorrow morning and we start the climb to Mt Stanley in the Ruwenzoris on 29th. (Ps! If you don't want to be on the list, remove yourself, I won't be offended:)

> **Vince Nixon:** Thanks.

> **Adrian Jardin:** Thanks Harry. No doubt you'll be posting pics/longer text updates on FB? Will you have data comms everywhere? Good luck all. Regards, Pigmy

> **Charmaine Manicom:** Good luck and enjoy y'all 😸

> **Paul Westcott:** Good luck! Have fun! Look forward to sharing vicariously 😃😃

> **Celeste Loots:** Looking forward to following your trip and seeing the photos:) Enjoy 😄

**HARRY:** Data coms may be sporadic at times, but more chance of getting a whatsapp message out than loading fb. Will post to fb whenever I get a decent connection. Pity you couldn't make it Adrian!

**Adrian Jardin**: Thanks, Yes, I'm jealous. I'll let you guys do the exploratory trip and then you can go again in a year or two :)

**Adrian Jardin**: BTW, for people who are worried about getting too many messages via whatsapp and they leave the group like one person did already, did you know you can "mute" a group and then go and look at the group messages only when you want to. I'll stop posting now!

**Fran Avery**: Good luck Harry, not that you'll need it! Have a great time! Xxx

**Bridgette Blackmore**: Have fun Harry :-) can I add you on facebook? Bxx

**Marinda Smit**: Enjoy!!!

**Richard Westcott**: What an adventure you have in front of you Cuz. Wishing you all the best, looking forward to following your quest!

**Sheila Swanepoel**: Enjoy! We are all in awe of yr energy and bravery. Lots of love

**Jèan-Prieur du Plessis**: Looking forward to follow the adventure! Peace ✌ brother.

**Azhar Butt**: Good luck Harry, looking forward to the updates and your adventure

**Barbara Wirz**: what a wonderful idea to keep us updated on your adventure like this... love to be part of the group!

**Vince Nixon**: And to think that it all started in Newcastle RSA.

**Sheila Swanepoel**: No! Harrismith's Platberg mountain started it all!

**Vince Nixon**: But you were in Newcastle at the time....

**HARRY:** Sheila's right, Vince. It was the mountain right on our doorstep where my love for mountains started... and of course the Drakensberg only a few kilometres hitch hike away :) Newcastle was the start of more organised trips...

**Vince Nixon**: I often talk about the hike that we did from the Memel pass to Mullers pass. But with my knee moanier now it is a thing of the past. It is the left knee. Need a replacement.

HARRY: Plastic knees... great idea for downhills, Vince... I've got pictures of our little epic into the unknown somewhere - will scan when i get back

**Vince Nixon**: Thanks. The photo will show how young and hansome we were. Now we are just hansome. But I still lead my Diehard soldiers into battle.

**Eileen MacFarlane**: Ian & I can never drive past Harrismith 'mountain' and not think of you Harry. From small beginnings to this awesome adventure, wow, most impressive. Eileen

**Theresa Rautenbach**: I agree with Sheila.  I'm totally in awe of your energy and zest for life.  have fun and please be safe 👀

**Vince Nixon**: By the way Harry, how old are you know??

HARRY: Surely you meant how young, Vince :) Not yet through adolescence at the tender age of six-zero...

**Vince Nixon**: Wow! Then I am ten years younger than you. But you have always been a very fit person. Goes with a fit brain.

HARRY: I'll be safe, Theresa, with the help of the people who live in the mountains, and my friend Andre who i have climbed with since the late 70s...

*Perfect start to the big adventure! Sunrise as i was leaving home this morning...*

**Paul Westcott:** 😊😊

**Megan MacFarlane:** Beautiful

HARRY: And ps! This message comes to you from 30,000 ft. Abusing the 15 mins free WiFi...

**Charles Barry:** Have fun

**Pepi Malamoglou:** Where? Enjoy

**Lee Bennett:** :)

**Vince Nixon:** God speed my friend.

HARRY: Somewhere above the dead Sea...

**Marinda Smit:** Whow!!!

**Celeste Loots:** Wonderful dawn for you:)

**Rob Campbell:** Hope the whole trip is everything you are looking forward to

**HARRY:** Cheers, Rob! Pity I couldn't have more of the old gang with me...

**Jean Landman** Climb every mountain search high and low....follow every rainbow..till you find your dream

**HARRY:** :)

**Pepi Malamoglou:** So the picture was dawn in England and you have WiFi in the sky😊😊

**Pepi Malamoglou:** What airline

**Jèan-Prieur du Plessis:** Thanks for sharing your adventure!

**HARRY:** Dawn at home/ WiFi in the sky / qatar... speak later

**Taron Lakhani:** 👍 🍫 xxxx

**Jose Simoes:** Beautiful view have fun and be safe

**Theresa Rautenbach:** A wonderful adventure ahead. Will keep you in my thoughts.

**Jo-Anne:** Stay safe and keep us posted ALL the time X

---

### 27 July 2016

**Thea Groenewegen:** Hi Harry, I am so jealous! Wish we we there! Have lots of fun! ⛺

**Matt Roderick:** There's a lot of "good luck" chatter and very few progress reports & pictures here. I'm hoping that changes soon, looking forward to seeing some awesomeness 😊😋😋😊

But "good luck" from me 😉

**Pepi Malamoglou:** Probably no Internet 😕

---

### 28 July 2016

**Ann Lake:** Good luck harry

**Roland Suhr**: Yes, concerned about the fate of Bwana Harry & his faithful askari "le Frog", who has to lug all this stuff.

**HARRY**: Bwana Harry and Askari Frog arrived late yesterday evening in their overnight abode. Woke this morning to find that our jungle camp is a place that Tarzan himself would have been happy to call home. Surrounded by large trees, waving palms and the song of birds, with the ever present Bulbul leading the chorus, and the sound of water rushing down the river, it is tranquil and a perfect place to relax after 30 hours of near continuous travel... Towering above our camp, is the mighty Ruwenzori. And although you can feel the presence of the mountain, she is living up to her nickname [reputation] and almost completely obscured by mist.

*My bungalow in the woods*

**Vince Nixon**: If you swing on any vines; look out for that tree; George...

**Charles Barry**: Just thump your chest and yell...Jane will appear

**HARRY**: I did thump my chest... she ran :)

**Charles Barry**: 😂

**Linette Simoes**: That looks awesome. Have a good rest before you continue on your adventure 😊

**Celeste Loots**: Looks like an idyllic place.

**Rob Campbell**: "Obscured by clouds" reminiscent of a wonderful Pink Floyd album!

**Rob Campbell**: Have you caught any Pokemons yet?

**Vince Nixon**: Dont spoil this area with Pokemons.

**Bridgette Blackmore**: Looks fantastic Tarzan :-)

**Jose Simoes**: Beautiful and enjoy it and stay safe

HARRY: Sounds like a perfect soundtrack for the mountain, Rob!

HARRY: What's a Pokemon?

**Pepi Malamoglou**: 😂😂😂😂

**Pepi Malamoglou**: Looks beautiful Harry. When do you start the trek?

**Rob Campbell**: The album was the sound track to a French film set in the New Guinea jungle. So maybe quite appropriate?

*Obscured by the clouds - in the background there is a mountain...*

**HARRY:** Set off tomorrow morning. On day 5, we'll stand on top of Margarita Pk (5109m), Africa's 3rd highest peak

**HARRY:** Interesting factoid Rob :)

**HARRY:** And btw... thanks for all the good wishes. I'll pass it on to André who has yet to discover whatsapp...

**HARRY:** Until next time I'm in reach of a signal :)

**Taron Lakhani:** Be safe. Love you dad

**Taron Lakhani:** Xxx

Pepi Malamoglou: 🙏🙏

**Paul Westcott:** Sounds too exciting! Hope Le Frog looks after the old chap 😄

**Theresa Rautenbach:** Climb the mountains Harry and get their good tidings 🙏

**Marinda Smit:** 👏👏👏👏

**Peter Winder:** Hi Harry, my very special friend. What an adventure! Have fun and come home safe.

Pete.

---

### 29 July 2016

**Ann Lake:** You are an inspiration Harry.   So looking forward  to following your adventures.   Thank you for including  me. Go well.   Ann

**HARRY:** 10km and a 1000 vertical metres later we've reached our first overnight stop. Nyabitabe Camp - which happens to be a hut - built on a ridge, with rivers rushing past on either side and an amazing view towards Portal Peak.  André and i have been joined by Mandy, a young lady i met in Ethiopian mountains, who was going to join us on Mt Kenya,  but since she was in the area socialising with gorillas, she's decided to join the two older reprobates on the trip up to Margaritha Peak.

*Portal Peak with the sun peeping through*

**Rob Campbell**: Sounds amazing. Enjoy fully.

**Rob Campbell**: 😃

**Jèan-Prieur du Plessis**: It looks like pleasant weather......curious what the temperatures are, low and high.

**Celeste Loots**: It's certainly lush and green there. Awesome view!

**Sheila Swanepoel**: So she's staying with the gorillas then? Hope she appreciates you two old silver backs.

**Sheila Swanepoel**: I'm just jealous.

**Adrian Jardin**: Good progress, 2,651m and counting ! I presume the temperature and humidity where you are now would be above my normal happy level 😃

**Pepi Malamoglou**: Traffic hectic and still need to stop by shops. Can you rather call tomorrow

**Pepi Malamoglou**: Sorry wrong person

**Ann Lake**: Hi harry beautiful photo of portal peak. What beautiful lush surrounding. Send photo of all of you. X Ann

**Ryan Loots**: We don't want them to break the camera lens.

**Ann Lake**: 😄

**Pepi Malamoglou**: 😄😄😄 especially the gorillas

**Taron Lakhani**: Ryan 😄

**Bridgette Blackmore**: Sounds amazing Harry and fantastic photo, very envious :-) Bx

**HARRY**: It's lush and green... the rain forest we climbed through is incredibly dense. Though where we're overnighting it's beginning to thin out as we start moving towards the bamboo region. Temperatures are still relatively mild where we are, though cooler than where we started, and enough humidity to have us all dripping as we were heading uphill... picture of gorillas and the fair maiden to follow...

**Barbara Wirz**: i should hope so :-)

*Mandy, Josephat (guide), yours truly, André*

**Jèan-Prieur du Plessis**:

**Theresa Rautenbach:** Have a good time Harry 🕊

**Jenny De Villiers:** 🧎 🍃 ♠ ♫ ⛰ 🔝

---

### 30 July 2016

**Ann Lake:** Harry  great to see photo of the gang.   Look forward  to daily update xann

---

### 01 August 2016

**HARRY:** After two days, most of which was spent walking in the Bujuku Valley, we're now approaching Elena Hut from where we'll launch our summit attempt early tomorrow morning.  The cloud cover lifted yesterday and for the first time we were able to see Margaritha Peak and the glacier that we have to cross to get to her! This morning we woke to a world covered in white. A reminder of how quickly the weather changes at altitude!! All of us are feeling the effects of altitude, with every upwards step an effort, leaving you out of breath, but with the summit in sight we're able to joke about it!

*John Matte Hut. Margaritha Peak (right) in the distance - the Elena Glacier at her feet*

*Crossing the Bigo Bog. Before the duck boards were installed people jumped from tussock to tussock. The guides tell that someone jumped, missed and fell in the bog never to be seen again...*

*Our world this morning. We breach the ridge at the notch, then traverse rightwards to Elena Hut*

**Adrian Jardin**: I see the hut is at 4,540 m. No wonder it's getting a bit thin up there ! Good luck and don't overdo it.

**Gerrit van der Merwe**: Mooiso en sterkte vir julle

**Rob Campbell**: All the best. Thinking of you

**Susan Nelson**: Good luck 🌸 xx

**Theresa Rautenbach**: Take care 🌿🌾🌴

**Sheila Swanepoel**: Enjoy Pikkie.

**Bridgette Blackmore**: Hi Harry, so good to hear about your expedition :-) It sounds very exciting :-) have just been reading that the Glaciers on your mountains have reduced by 50% in the last half century......

**Jèan-Prieur du Plessis**: Vasbyt!

**Paul Westcott**: Great! Well done but no rush. Take care!

**Bridgette Blackmore**: Great pic :-)

**Jose Simoes**: Well done and good luck. Have fun and be safe

**Sheila Swanepoel:** Charming! Well then just watch yr bloody step!

**Bridgette Blackmore:** Oh my, looks like quite a long board walk as well! Take care but have fun :-)

**Charles Barry:** Lekka!!!

**Marinda Smit:** Go for it!! There is No Turnback😎😎

*View from the hut...*

*The 'hut'. The glacier we have to climb on the right...*

**Adrian Jardin**: Hope your crampons are sharp and watch out for the crevasses !

**HARRY:** Thanks for all the care and wishes! We will take care and try to give the crevasses a wide berth. More news tomorrow...

**Ann Lake:** Oh Harry I am in awe. It is spectacular albeit frightening. Tread carefully , cautiously and consciously. Am so enjoying sharing your adventure.

---

### 02 August 2016

---

**HARRY:** 04.51... we're nearly ready to go. It's pitch dark and somewhere in the near distance below us, a tremendous thunderstorm is playing out. Above us stars.

**HARRY:** 08.11... at the base of the Margaritha glacier. The last obstacle between us and the summit

*Getting crampons etc on...*

*Made it...*

**Celeste Loots:** Looks wonderful Harry. I'm in the Umfolozi game reserve enjoying the bush. Take care and enjoy. What a memorable experience! Great pics

**Paul Westcott:** Woo hoo 😊😊

**Charles Barry:** Strongs

**Rob Campbell:** Well done

**Theresa Rautenbach:** 👏👏👏😄😄😄

**Rob Campbell:** 🙌

**Jèan-Prieur du Plessis:** 👏👏👏 👍👍👍

**Bridgette Blackmore:** Awesome! Well done guys :-) xx lovely photos :-)

**Sheila Swanepoel:** Well done Pikkie. Knew you could do it! What a wonderful achievement. Lots of love

**Azhar Butt:** Well done Harry

**Jo-Anne:** 👏👏👏 well done :-) love from all of us xxxxx

**Ann Lake**: Awesome Harry  congrats 1 down (or up) 2  to go.  Love Ann

**Barbara Wirz**: bravissimi!

congratulations xxxxxxx

**Megan MacFarlane**: What an awesome and inspiring achievement. Congrats and love from all the MacFarlanes

**Julie-Anne Moors**: Well Done!

**Paul Westcott**: Fantastic! Well done

**Paul Behrens**: Brilliant Harry! And thanks for taking us wannabe travelers along in spirit.

**Taron Lakhani**: Well done dad. XXXX

**Jenny De Villiers**: Well done to you all. Great achievement! The saying, "If you reach for the sky, then you're short sighted" sure rings true to you. You definitely go for far greater heights!

**Vince Nixon**: Well done Harry! What was on the other side of the mountain???

**Adrian Jardin**: The DRC

**Gerrit van der Merwe**: Mooiso Harry!!

**Thea Groenewegen**: Ons is trots op jou! Baie geluk Harry.

**Jose Simoes**: Congrats you guy's well done.

**Susan Nelson**: Congratulations !!! xx

*First light yesterday morning... have to get across all that snow to Margaritha on the far right...*

*Geared up to tackle the glacier*

*Step. Step. Rest...*

Harry Loots

*Beautiful, precarious traverse.*

**HARRY**: Thank you! Appreciate all your support and love!!

*Woke next to Lake Kithandara this morning*

**HARRY**: Conversation with one of the guides from another group we had met a few days ago: "How was the peak?"... "Beautiful!"... "that's good! We were praying for you!" They're an amazing, caring group of people; the people who make it possible for us to reach these heights!!

**Peter Winder**: Hi Harry

I'm following your progress and am in awe of your achievements so far. I'll keep watching as long as you guys keep climbing!

Pete.

**Pepi Malamoglou**: 🏆🏆🥂🥂👏👏👏 well done Harry and team. Take care coming down and rest before the next one😊😊😊

**Ryan Loots**: Thought you were young and fit 😊 you should be running up 😊

**Jo-Anne**: As beautiful as it all looks, please stay safe :-) X

**Jose Simoes**: Awesome enjoy and stay safe

**Theresa Rautenbach**: So inspiring.  Be safe 😊

*Changing landscape*

**Paul Westcott**: Looks amazing but hard work. Well done and stay safe!

**Eileen MacFarlane**: An awesome achievement! Be safe and tread with care.

**Jèan-Prieur du Plessis**: Simply AMAZING! What a feat! Congratulations.

**Celeste Loots**: Can't believe how icy it is up there! Brrr! Glad you're meeting caring people on your journey 🙏 All looks awesome.

**Linette Simoes**: Well done to you all. Stay safe and enjoy😊

**Roland Suhr**: Was worried that Bwana Harry might end up in a big pot & askari le Frog be adopted as a mascot by the Pygmies. But glad to see that all hazards overcome by the intrepid pair.

**Barbara Wirz**: what a beautiful anecdote (conversation with the guide)! and it takes one to appreciate the beauty in them! xxx

**Anke Hafmans**: Well done Harry! Looks amazing! 😎🤗

*Steep descent yesterday to 2651m through some great scenery. The sooner you get low, the sooner the body starts recovering...*

**Paul Westcott:** Beautiful scenery!

**Charles Barry:** ☺

**Bridgette Blackmore**: Amazing landscapes Harry :-)

**Marinda Smit:** 👏👏👏

**Gerrit van der Merwe**: Baie mooi

**Roland Suhr**: As usual, pictures well-composed & informative Harry. But what about some "back story"? Tell us about the fellow trudging along in gumboots with the awkward-looking load on his back. One of your porters? How many times a day does he go up & down? What does a trip earn him in USD?

HARRY: A short hike this morning brought us back to the park gates where we started. Lots of praise and congratulations from the park staff and certificates to mark our achievement! It is an amazing experience to be standing 5km above sea level, and a privilege to have the opportunity to do so. Doing so without the support of the porters (one of which, Amon, with the awkward load, shepherded me on the non-technical parts of the trip), and the guides, would make this even more difficult than it is. Sadly, as Roland probably guessed, they are exploited! I discovered yesterday that they earn 10000 Ugandan shillings - less than 3 usd per day... (compare this to minimum wage on Mt Kenya of about 20 usd per day). I also know that what we are paying the tour company should earn them a lot more than that!!! Even sadder is the fact that this exploitation is by their own people! Guides, who put their lives at risk to protect us, don't fare much better, getting about 10 usd per day!

A few observations...

At 5000m I was walking and chewing on an energy bar... a quarter energy bar to be exact... I had to stop after a few steps to catch my breath... who would have thought the simple process of chewing could be that hard...

Peeling a boiled egg yesterday, I noticed that I was leaving black muddy dispenser finger marks on the white egg... then it went in my mouth without a further thought...

This morning, we were all brought to near tears when we found out that Ronald, the assistant chef's brother had died yesterday! It didn't stop him from preparing our breakfast. And he would have carried on serving us if i didn't send him home...

We passed by the family home on our way to Kasese. Hundreds of people were gathering for the funeral. All expecting to be fed for taking the trouble to attend the funeral. A cow and several goats will be slaughtered to feed the masses. The burial party get a goat of their own. As does the senior uncle of the departed...

Prior our adventure, Mandy had never walked with crampons or held an ice axe, let alone climb a solid ice wall, and despite admitting to wanting to cry and/or be sick on a few occasions, and particularly on an exposed traverse, made it to the top and back...

I'm also left wondering if my mother's warnings about not washing my hands after I've been to the toilet will come true :)

**Celeste Loots**: Hard to hear these snippets Harry. Have you started a sponsoring site for your 3 peaks challenge? It's a good opportunity with all the people following your adventure:)

**Leslie Kett**: Harry. Take care brother

**Jose Simoes**: Enjoy it and stay safe

**Lee Bennett**: You really should write a book Harry when you've got time. :0)

**Ann Lake**: So enjoying your descriptions. The scenery is spectacular. Xxann

**Theresa Rautenbach**: Hope you'll have a good night's rest Harry and stay safe

**Thea Groenewegen**: Hi Harry, congratulations! Another peak in the bag! So sorry to hear about your porter's bad fortune. It just reminds a person how vulnerable the poor are. Hope you enjoy the rest of your trip! 💯!!

**Pepi Malamoglou**: Keep it up Harry and I agree with Lee. Write a book 😊😊

**Marinda Smit**: Congrats Harry!!! Well done👏👏👏👏👏

**Ryan Loots**: FYI: 'We're going to be out of reach for a few days. Heading to Shipton camp. Harry'

**Rob Campbell**: Sterkte and joy!

**Bridgette Blackmore**: Have fun :-) happy trails 😄

**Charles Barry**: 😇

**Megan MacFarlane**: Safe Travels

**Roland Suhr**: Haya Safari!

**Vince Nixon**: Hi Harry.

Waiting for all the photos on face book. Then I can see them on a big screen.

HARRY: Monday: After two days of travelling, from Uganda to Nanyuki in Kenya we started walking in the afternoon and reached our first overnight camp, Old Moses just as it started raining  (this is the 'dry season', btw).

HARRY: Tuesday: we started in the rain, managed to get our raincoats off for half an hour and then spent the next 4 plus hours in a freezing rain... Mandy (who's rejoined André and I), and I, arrived at Shipton's Camp in a half frozen state. Our porters and thus our warm clothes would take another two hours to get here... i had a thin jumper on and (fortunately) my jacket in my daypack. With my jumper plus the thin jacket she had, my rain pants and socks on she had at least some warmth. And so did I. Mahendra, a German who was in Old Moses the night before filled his water bottle with hot water and gave it to Mandy for her to warm herself. With her feet on top of the bottle and me sitting behind her back we managed to warm her a few degrees. Great was our joy when our warm clothes finally arrived. Great was my dismay when I discovered that my clothes had wet patches on. But, wet patches or not they would still make me a 100-times warmer than what I was. So, on they went. A couple of hot brews later we crawled into our sleeping bags for more warmth, staying there until dinner was served.

---

### 10 August 2016

**Jèan-Prieur du Plessis:** 😄😄 hope you get better weather going forward.

**Bridgette Blackmore:** A bit if a chilly tale but It sounds like a great adventure story unfolding. Keep safe and warm 😊

**Barbara Wirz:** wish i could send you some of sicily's redundant heat and drought... stay safe xxxxx

**Theresa Rautenbach:** Hope you will be able to sleep well and warm tonight and wish you guys lovely sunny weather tomorrow.

**Celeste Loots:** What a chilly ordeal, but glad to know Mandy is being looked after:)

**Sheila Swanepoel:** Hell Pikkie you certainly are being tested. Really admire you. I would phone my mum after the first raindrop. Keep warm. Love

**Ann Lake:** Whew Harry. Rain-chilled bones take some time to warm up. Hope weather improves. What an adventure. Be safe and warm. Regards Ann

**Paul Westcott:** Keep warm Cuz

Tomorrow will be better we all hope! Mandy must have been finished!

Keep safe

**Charles Barry:** I remember a boy scout troop in the normandien mountains cold and wet ...drinking tea made from pine needles.

**Charles Barry:** ☺

**Jean Landman:** Safe and warm wishes

**Paul Behrens:** Haha, had forgotten that episode of Scout Adventures with Charles & Harry. Best of luck with the rest of your climb Harry

---

## 11 August 2016

**HARRY:** Wednesday: i went outside after dinner on Tuesday evening and there was a dazzling display of stars, lifting spirits and hope for clear weather! Alas, it was not to be. Wednesday morning started with the peaks once again wrapped in layers of clouds. We'd agreed with Moses to go to Pt Lenana at 09.00 this morning, but with the clouds as low as they were and visibility zero, we delayed. Eventually at 10, Moses set off with André and Mandy. My pack etc were still sopping wet, so i stayed behind to try and get them dry and start writing that book everyone has been mentioning...

**HARRY:** Wednesday about 14.00. It has now rained some more, the cloud cover has thickened and a strong wind is blowing. I have a chat with Duncan, and we agree that a) this being the dry season the rain is likely to last for another 2 days (3-4 days is typical for wet spells during the dry season), and b) the combination of mist / rain cloud plus strong winds will result in the rock freezing over. We agree to call of the climb and retreat from the mountain, which would then enable us to rearrange Kilimanjaro timetable and come back after to climb Batian. Despite the lateness of the afternoon and knowing that if we leave now it would mean walking in the dark for part of the way, I'm freezing and decide that a couple of hours of headlamp walking with a warm hut with 1) fireplace 2) warm shower 3) cold beer, beats sitting and shivering in our current hut without any of the abovementioned attractions... Duncan looks equally keen to get going so we decide to leave at 4pm on what's supposed to be a 6-7 hour walk. Andre is not keen on walking in the dark and happy to spend the night. Mandy wants to come along but decides that she'll slow us up and decides to stay. So, now should i go on my own? Or stay? I decide that I've shivered enough for one day/week/month... the walk in the dark is a minor tradeoff by comparison. So we set off. Duncan and I with two porters Simon and Boneface. And a bag of maize meal and some veg to make a sauce/stew to eat with the ugali (putu for my South African friends). We're at the 'roadhead' at 8pm, 4 hours after we set off and now less than 45 mins away from the bandas. The path is very wet and slippery, and we're forced to go slower. Near the river Duncan starts hitting his walking sticks together to warn away stray buffalo and elephant bulls who are known to roam this area. We don't come across any (i was wondering which of the gang i would have to outrun, if we were chased... :) and shortly after, at 9.30pm we arrive at the bandas, greeted by a herd of buffalo, and Jarvin the hut keeper and his helper Washington... in a few minutes the fire's on the go, the shower is ready and the beers are on their way...

*The gorgeous Gorges Valley (and the rest of Kenya) covered in cloud. (We had about 15mins of clear sky just as the sun was setting, on our descent)*

Harry Loots

*Lake Michealson at sunset with clouds rolling back in. The rest of our descent was in cloud and soon after this was taken, in darkness...*

*Having a very deserved beer with Boneface and Simon. All three were just as happy as i was to be in a warm hut with a fireplace and moaning together about the lack of fire at Shipton's camp where we had left from...*

**HARRY:** Footnote: Boneface is pronounced bonnie face, and not bone face which may be an obvious name for the young man,  given his high cheekbones... he and Simon are close friends. Simon is probably a real lady-killer. Tall and well built he stands out amongst his peers. He's training under Duncan to be a guide and hopes to shortly go to Germany for climbing training. Duncan I've known for some time and think of him as a friend, despite the client/guide relationship while we're on the mountain! Solid and dependable, we see things in a similar way making for a great mountaineering partnership. And somewhat ironically, a few of you having asked about fundraising, this is the one place where I would like to help raise funds for. The training/advanced training of guides. More on that later...

**HARRY:** One final thought on this chapter, while waiting for Andre and Mandy to join me. While we were walking in the dark yesterday evening, Boneface slipped and I caught him, stopping him from falling. It struck me that at that point in time the roles of client, guide, porters no longer existed. Tomorrow when I pay them, they'll come back into play, but right then we were just four men making our way off a mountain. Class, colour, culture, any differences we may have, disappearing into the mists that surrounded us...

**Sheila Swanepoel**: Was that Charles Ryder?

**Pepi Malamoglou**: Thanks so much for sharing your adventures with us. Keeping you and your team in prayer throughout your travels. 🙏🙏❤️❤️

**Charles Barry**: Much blessing

**Jo-Anne**: Thinking of you all, please stay. Love you x

**Jean Landman**: Be safe please

**Paul Westcott**: Such a wonderful story !

Keep it up and safe travels 😊😊

**Sheila Swanepoel**: He'll Pikkie Mrs Bedford would be proud of yr descriptive writing. I love reading yr account. Love

**Jean Landman**: The sentence of class, colour and race must be the foreword

**Bridgette Blackmore**: It's amazing and a privilege to read  your accounts of your adventure Harry :-)  take care :-)

**Ryan Loots** changed this group's icon

---

### 12 August 2016

**Thea Groenewegen**: This sounds like Harry's style of hiking! Never a dull moment!

**Linette Simoes**: Wonderful 👍

HARRY: Sheila, I think Mrs Bedford may have slapped me around the ears a few times for deliberately breaking all kinds of grammatical rules :) I would have hoped that she would nevertheless have enjoyed reading about our journey!

HARRY: Ps! Charles Barry. Friend and fellow Scoutmaster, Newcastle's finest 1st Troop in the late 70s, early 80s. Paul, who mentioned Charles, was a senior Scout and a friend ever since.

One of the huts at Meru Bandas, where i retreated to from the cold, draped in a cloud of mist. I stayed here before in 2008, and always thought this would be the perfect hideaway if you wanted to escape from cities... no electricity, no mobile network, no WiFi. Buffalo graze on the lawns at night, elephant gather at the watering hole a few hundred metres below.

More early morning mist at Meru Bandas

**Theresa Rautenbach**: Beautiful.  Bigly warm hugs from Zululand 🌱

**Gerrit van der Merwe**: Nice Harry...enjoy

**Jean Landman**: Love from Cape Town

**Celeste Loots**: Very atmospheric in the mists. Enjoy the day

**Pepi Malamoglou**: Hugs from joburg

**Vince Nixon**: Hand shake from Newcastle...

HARRY: By the way... many thanks for all the ongoing well-wishes. It's great to know friends are continuously supporting and motivating from afar. Love and hugs to all. (And Vince, after all these years i think we can move from the formal handshake to a man-hug 😄)

**Bronwyn MacFarlane**: Lots of love xxx your pictures look amazing xxx

HARRY: Ps! Re the pine needles episode... I've discovered there was nothing wrong with our theory of infusing tea with pine needles to make up for the lack of sugar... the only thing we did wrong, I've discovered in the Dolomites, is that you should infuse the pine needles (mugo) in Grappa.

*At the equator, a few days ago*

**Bronwyn MacFarlane:** 👍

*Hall's Tarn with various minor peaks in the background. The base of Pt Lenana is on the right.*

**Jose Simoes:** 👍👍

**Jèan-Prieur du Plessis**: Still having a great time following your journey! It's like watching the Harry Olympics. Please refresh our memories what the rest of the planned timetable looks like.

**HARRY:** At the time i was reading the mention of Scouts, I was travelling past Nyeri in Kenya. I remembered much later that Nyeri is the burial place of Baden-Powell... coincidence...

*J-P, at this minute I'm sitting in the very peaceful and rustic lounge/restaurant of the Mountain Inn, a few km from Moshi.*

**HARRY**: Spent the morning arranging our Kilimanjaro programme. Agreed daily plans with senior guide and menus with cook (they'll bring bread to the table 3 times a day, so 'guidance' is useful...). We are using the Umbwe Route via the Western Breach, sleeping in the crater, immediately below the summit, on our final night before we start our descent off the mountain. I'll post updates as and when i get a signal...

**Jèan-Prieur du Plessis**: Wonderful! Enjoy every minute. 🐚

**Paul Westcott**: Meru sounds idyllic!

Thanks for sharing your experiences and be safe on Kili. Will be waiting with bated breath for the next exciting episode in your odyssey!

---

### 14 August 2016

---

**Bridgette Blackmore**: Hope all goes well Harry, it all sounds very exciting and challenging. Hope this leg doesn't get too cold 😊 Enjoy 😊

**HARRY**: Having a last cup of tea before we travel to Umbwe Gate in Kilimanjaro national park, where we start today's trek. Mandy has now gone off possibly down the East coast of Kenya towards Zanzibar and then eventually further on South Africa. So it's Andre and i on this climb with a team of about 10 guides, cook and porters. I woke this morning realising that this is a BIG mountain! What she lacks in technical challenges, she more than makes up for in height... by the time we summit, we'll have climbed nearly 5 vertical kilometres! which feels like a long long way right now...

**Pepi Malamoglou**: Strength Harry and Andre and your team. What is your ETA to the top?

**Theresa Rautenbach**: Good luck and bigly hugs 🫂

**HARRY**: On day 4 (Thursday, we'll be in the crater (5800m). If we're feeling strong, we'll go to the summit in the afternoon (5895m). If we're tired, or the weather is bad, we'll summit the next morning.

**Roland Suhr:** Haya Safari Bwana Harry & Askari Andre!⤴

**HARRY:** Asante sana! (Thank you very much)

**Berkan Özden:** Good luck Harry!

**Jean Landman:** 👍

*Ryan thinks his dad's efforts of nearly 5000 vertical metres are feeble... he does 5000 in a day on his bicycle :)*

**Pepi Malamoglou:** 😅😅😅

**Rob Campbell:** Enjoy this immensely. And hope all goes safely.

**Barbara Wirz:** the apple doesn't fall far from the tree😊

**HARRY:** Except the apple needs wheels to get up hills :)

**Charles Barry:** Strongs

*Umbwe Gate - starting point*

**Mandy:** 😄

**Paul Westcott:** 

**Gerrit van der Merwe:** go Harry

*Our trail through the indigenous rain forest. Trees taller than buildings. All shapes and sizes.*

*As we approached the campsite, we started moving above the clouds (2800+m) and saw the sun for the first time today*

**HARRY:** Our campsite (Umbwe Cave) last night turned out to to be superb. The moon, on its way to being full cast a light glow over our tents (a personal tent each, plus shared mess and toilet tent. (Btw, we think we may have the special treat of a full moon when we sleep on top - massive consolation for having to abandon Mt Kenya.) During the night Colobus Monkeys were heard regularly during the night, sometimes right above us. Waking to the sound of birds, a perfect start to what is turning out to be gloriously sunny day. Well for us at any rate, where we are above the clouds.

**HARRY:** After breakfast this morning we were introduced to the crew. Gideon is chief guide, Willy 2ic. Then there's Ally the chef, Mgaya, chef's helper and waiter, and Edwin (whom i dubbed the 'chemical engineer' - he has the unenviable task of cleaning the portable toilets every morning) and another 7 porters... after the introductions we were treated to some singing - including a modified version of jambo bwana (think Lion King)...

> **Pepi Malamoglou:** Stunning. Thanks for sharing, hope you get the full moon when you summit

**HARRY:** Snack break at about 3600m in a typical heather zone. Higher than the Drakensberg, and another 200m to our campsite. While walking through the beautiful rain forest, i said to Andre that I'm beginning to think i should have come here a long time ago... the forest is totally enchanting. Yellow trees, olive trees, huge tree ferns and a host of other grand old trees.

*View from the snack spot*

*She's put a spell on me....*

**Paul Westcott:** 😊😊😊

*Barranco Camp at the head of the Barranco Valley.*

**HARRY:** Last night it was only Andre and my tents, and another small group a little before us. This campsite being at a junction of three routes (Machame, Lemosho and Umbwe), you could end up with a few hundred people (including porters) here on any night! A tent village! Our tents are on the extreme left. Apparently people on the Umbwe Route are pitched apart from the rest... on Snob Hill?

> **Jèan-Prieur du Plessis:** Thank you for sharing as your memories are made.

> **Thea Groenewegen:** Wish I was there! It brings back a lot of memories! Have lots of fun and good weather! 🏔️🏞️

> **Jose Simoes:** Thanks for keeping us posted. stay safe and have fun.

**HARRY**: While having our lunch yesterday afternoon, I looked up, saw a large bird gliding towards our mess tent, suddenly realised it was a Bearded vulture, got very excited, ran outside, and called Andre to come and watch this magnificent creature gliding past - less than 10m, and almost directly above us - so close that I could clearly see the beard that gives rise to its other name, 'Bearded Vulture'. It continued down along the spur of the valley we were camping on. At the bottom of the spur the wing tips turned up, braking and then it turned 180° and continued up the left bank of the adjacent spur, doing another 180° turn at the apex before gliding down the right bank, flying so low, and being so well camouflaged, that had we not been able to see its shadow on the shrubs and plants below, we would not have known it was there. One more turn took it up the next spur and then it was gone...

**HARRY**: A balmy sunny afternoon ended in a very rapid temperature drop to about 4 or 5°C, with both Andre and I donning long johns and adding extra layers before sitting down at the dinner table. A little drop of Johnny Walker raised the inner temperature and the warm soup and chapattis did the rest. I crawled into my sleeping bag. Somewhere around midnight I woke and after debating with myself whether I should use the pee bottle or not decided to venture into the cold to look at the stars. With the moon nearly full the mountain looked stunningly beautiful and I once again asked myself why I haven't made this trip before...

## 17 August 2016

**HARRY**: Wednesday: our camp is pitched on a small shelf, which according to Gideon was covered in ice about a foot thick as little as fifteen years ago. Now the only remaining glacier is a patch on the left-hand side and below the rocky ridge we have to breach tomorrow to reach the crater. A few other patches cling doggedly to the crevices of the ridge. It was the melting of some of these patches which caused a rockslide in 2006, killing 5 or 6 climbers and porters (I don't remember all the details so if someone wants to check and update, please do). The route was closed for a few years while an investigation was held and eventually reopened along a safer and more protected passage. Sadly it has retained a reputation as being a dangerous route. (Every route on Kilimanjaro has the potential for rockfall, and lives have been claimed on other routes, too, but not 5 or 6 at the same time.) On the bright side, this means that very few parties come along this Western Breach route. Which in turn meant that while the campsite at Barranco may have had as many as 500 people camping, last night and tonight Andre and I together with our teams are the only people at our campsite. And what magnificent campsites both have been. Last night we camped next to Lava Tower. In the afternoon we scaled the tower with Willy and Suleimon, one of the porters, who looked ever so eager when i asked if any of them want to join us. He's a bright and friendly young lad who wants to become a guide. He is the only Muslim in the group, and soon after we had set up camp this afternoon he took his sleeping mat and went to do his prayers on a rock outcrop just above us. A few of which I'd like to think was for our safe passage tomorrow.

---

### 18 August 2016

**Ryan Loots:** From **HARRY:** On our way to Arrow Glacier Camp. Not had much signal.

---

### 19 August 2016

**Pepi Malamoglou:** Thanks Ryan. They're in my prayers 🙏

**Barbara Wirz:** thank you, ryan. they're in my thoughts, too...

**Anita Henning:** ...and in mine...

**Bridgette Blackmore:** Good to have some news and wishing them well 😊

**Celeste Loots**: What happened with them reaching the summit of Kilimanjaro at full moon ? 😐 I was looking at the moon here and thinking of them.

**Taron Lakhani**: From Harry. Off the mountain. Speak later.  xxx

**Jean Landman**: 😃

**Paul Westcott**: 😊😊

**Barbara Wirz**: 🙏

**Jean Landman**: So beautiful thanks for taking us with you on your journey

**Bridgette Blackmore**: Just wow!! 😊 love reading your accounts Harry :-)

**Thea Groenewegen**: Dit klink heerlik! Julle is teen hierdie tyd seker goed geaklimatiseer. Word julle geaffekteer deur die hoogte?

HARRY: Quick update: we made our way up the Western Breach route yesterday morning and arrived at our campsite in the crater at 10.30. After doctoring one of our porters who was suffering from altitude sickness, Gideon, André and I set off for the summit, arriving at 11.59 am. This morning we visited the very impressive Reusch Crater and the ash pit before making our way of the mountain - all the way out to Mweku Gate... a super hard day, but definitely worth the extra few hours on your feet to get into a hot shower!

*On the summit with Gideon*

*Full moon rising over Uhuru Peak*

**Thea Groenewegen:** Congratulations Harry and Frog! Wow, quite impressive to summit and walk to Mweku Gate, all in one day! You must have a Kilimanjaro beer on my behalf! 💯!!

**HARRY**: Thanks Thea :) Frog (André) has already disappeared to his bed... warm, no tent flapping in a hundred mile hour wind and even better,  no waking up in the middle of the night wondering where the next breath is... and when I've finished my Kilimanjaro beer shandy I'm going to be off to my bed as well.

**Celeste Loots**: 👐🤙💧😊😄

**Thea Groenewegen**: Enjoy your well deserved rest! 😴🛏️🤙

**Paul Westcott**: Congratulations on a job well done! Proud of you!

**Rob Campbell**: Well done

**Ryan Loots** changed this group's icon

**Jèan-Prieur du Plessis**: 👍👍👏👏

**Gerrit van der Merwe**: Well done guys...absolutely  awesome 🍺🍺

**Pepi Malamoglou**: Well done 👏👏🤙🤙

**Leslie Kett**: https://youtu.be/noUs3NfC07o

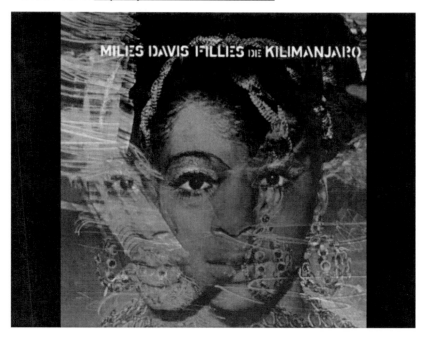

**Anita Henning**: Well done - another one hits the dust.

**Bridgette Blackmore**: I've just been looking at Kili on Google earth. It looks Incredible!!

**Bridgette Blackmore**: Fantastic adventure Harry :-)

**Vince Nixon**: How many more do you plan on doing. I just completed a 2,5km walk with my dog.

**Pepi Malamoglou**: 😂😂

**Thea Groenewegen**: That is a good start! 😊

**Theresa Rautenbach**: My phone's been stolen so missed out on news. But am back online 😊

Watched Everest the movie last night and thought of you

**HARRY**: A few final notes on this chapter...

Thursday morning, 05.00: Gideon or Willy taps on the tent and says morning. When i respond he moves on to Andre's tent and does the same. On previous days we didn't move from our warm sleeping bags until the sun reached our camp. Somewhere between 08.00 and 08.30. And didn't start walking until after 10.00 the day before. Today however the cold that we avoided on previous days is our friend!

The Western Breach Route follows a line through the western rock barrier below Uhuru Peak. This rock barrier is a precariously stacked pile of blocks of various sizes piled on top of each other forming tall pillars, 'glued' together with a layer of ice. Stacked side by side they resemble organ pipes, but without the smoothness. At night time the temperature drops and the ice expands, pushing the blocks apart a little fraction at a time. Next day as the outer layer of ice turns into water it flows down and fills the gap caused by the expansion. Next night this water freezes and expands, repeating the action of pushing the blocks apart. So, at the same time as the ice is trying its best to hold the pile of blocks together, it is also trying its best to push them apart. Fortunately while it's cold the rock pile is in a fairly stable state. But as the sun warms the rocks, those that have been pushed apart to the point where they are overbalancing, are released and tumble down. This has resulted in an area of a few hundred metres that has been demarcated as a 'rockfall corridor', i.e., where the greatest incidence of falling rocks occur. A danger zone. It is this rockfall corridor that you must cross early morning, while the ice is holding it together, to reduce the risk of rock being hurled at you.

And so, despite the sign that informs that you must leave before 05.30, at about 06.15 Gideon, Willy, André and i set off on the path that leads up and through the Western Breach. The porters are in the process of breaking camp and will be following soon, and overtaking us before too long. The wind is screaming at us and within a few hundred metres my fingers are frozen. The kind of frozen that's so sore that you want to bite your fingertips off. And it doesn't take long for my toes to reach the same stage. I'm constantly on the alert for any sounds of rock falling. Constantly on the lookout for large boulders that i might be able to dive behind if a rock tries to attack me. Constantly keeping an eye on my three companions. Our combined alertness can make the difference between being hit or missed if there is a rockfall. Inwardly, quietly sighing as we reach the 'rock train', a vertical rib of rock, providing cover and protection from potential rockfall above. We stop for a water break while our porters with loads of 20kg balanced on their heads, icicles formed on their upper lips stream past.

Higher up, we stop again for a cup of thick black sugary coffee and some biscuits that Willy digs out of his bag. I squirt an energy gel into my mouth and have a few bites of energy bar. Not too much, as the chewing leaves me breathless. (Almost every movement at this altitude leaves you breathless. Turning in your sleeping bag. Pulling your boots on. Tying your shoelaces. Unzipping the tent. Going to the toilet.) Then we're off again. Uhuru Peak looming above us and getting nearer until finally we break through the last rock band and a short diagonal walk later we're in the crater. Four and a quarter hours after we started. High fives, handshakes and hugs are exchanged. To our left we have a glacier that looks like a giant iceberg. On our right, the crater rim on which Uhuru Peak sits. And in front of us a large sandpit that we have to cross to get to our campsite.

*The Western Breach Route - following the diagonal rib that breaches the rock barrier at its narrowest point into the crater.*

*Sunset, the evening before we ascended the breach. Mt Meru peeping out of the clouds.*

*The remaining glacier near our camp in the crater. [edited: Furtwangler Glacier, Northern Icefields in background]*

**Theresa Rautenbach**: Beautiful

**Celeste Loots**: Wow! Is this all on Kilimanjaro?

**Ann Lake**: You write so well Harry.  So enjoying  your epic  journey.

**Harry**: All Kilimanjaro! Amazingly diverse. So many different facets.

**Harry**: Thanks Ann! Glad you're enjoying it :)

**Harry**: Sad event, Theresa. Some of my climbing friends were on the mountain at the time, all came away safely.

**Harry**: Thursday 11.00. To the summit. After finding some ibuprofen in my bag to doctor one of our porters who is complaining of a serious headache, Gideon, André and i set off for the summit. We'd already gained about 850 vertical metres today and this last nearly 150 metres turns out to be extra tough going. Tough enough for André to comment when we get to the top that a winch would have been useful...

At 11.59 we reach the signboard that tells you you have reached the top of Africa. Nothing special about it. Just another mountain top.

And yet, once again, as I look around me at the scenery, the Reusch Crater to my left, Mawenzi below and in front of me, the Southern ice fields to my right, a clear blue sky above, and a sign behind me that says you've made it, I wonder, with a little more emotion than I'd care to admit, why i waited so long to climb Kilimanjaro!

Harry Loots

*The remaining Southern ice fields. Mt Meru in the background.*

**Celeste Loots**: And was the full moon visible?

**Pepi Malamoglou**: Stunning views and pictures. Once again huge congratulations on this amazing achievement Harry and Andre. Bravo

---

### 23 August 2016

---

**Jose Simoes**: Congrats on another achievement to you and the team. Thanks for keeping us posted. Well done

**Roland Suhr**: Must tip my sola topi in the direction of Bwana Harry & Askari le Frog. Well done chaps! But must remind you that it remains a 3 Peaks Adventure. Are you curling back to knock off Mt Kenya, as I seem to remember as Plan B or does it remain like the Königsberg 7 Bridge Problem, unsolved? Of course, winkling is Frog out of the Business Class Lounge, where he'a discovered a supply of Tullamore Dew or Jameson's, may pose a problem, but it can be overcome by the necessary disciplinary measures.

**HARRY:** The Ash Pit and descending...

As if sleeping in the crater at an altitude of about 5734m wasn't going to be difficult enough, with temperatures in the minus teens, we were battered by a wind that threatened to rip the tent from the ground at times. Making our night even more memorable, was the fact that we had accidentally ended up with old tents that had various things wrong with them. Zips sometimes closed. Sometimes they didn't. Other times they'd pull apart and leave gaps. Tiny holes in the tent wall through which the wind whistled and tormented. Manageable at lower altitudes, but a constant source of discomfort at this altitude.

Fortunately the sun reaches the crater much earlier than the western side we had ascended and by 7 we were both out of our tents and ready to go. We told Ally to keep breakfast simple. Coffee and scrambled eggs. Gas cookers do not operate efficiently at any altitude... and apart from the two of us, he had 13 other people to feed... Mgaya, porter, cook's helper, waiter and chief hugger whenever we arrived at a new destination, most apologetically announced that the milk was finished when he brought us our flask of coffee. Thick. Black. And full of sediment, possibly thanks to a much lower boiling point (we estimated boiling point would have been somewhere around 80 degrees at this altitude).

Gideon, our chief guide, in addition to the chest infection he developed (I'd had him on antibiotics for two days by this time), had also developed symptoms of altitude sickness - headache, nausea, upset stomach, so we told him to pack and get going off the mountain asap, and wait for us at Barrafu camp about a 1000m lower. And so shortly after 7.30 am, Andre, Willy and I set off for the Ash Pit. Pole, pole, one last time, as we slowly made our way up the crater wall. As we topped the crater rim, we were hit by a wind of jetspeed proportion that tried its utmost to blow us back where we had come from. And with the wind came a very strong smell of sulphur. Like the smell of rotten eggs. Sickening. Nauseating. And dangerous. Fortunately we were on a level patch and could speed away

Harry Loots

from the sulphurous gas quite quickly. Safely away from the gas, we had time to start enjoying this amazing left-over from a volcanic eruption that happened more than 200,000 years ago. The inner core is a near perfect concentric funnel, surrounded by a level valance containing a mixture of lava rock, sulphur, volcanic sand, sedimentary rocks, etc... some of it looking like it had been shot from a cannon, others as if it had been neatly arranged in long arching rows. Due to the strong wind which must have pushed the temperature into the minus twenties or below we didn't go all the way to the inner core, skirting the edge of the valance before making our way out of the crater and onto its rim, then circumnavigating it, while making our way towards Stella Point, from where we would start our descent off the mountain. We had decided that if we go well on our descent that we'd go all the way to the gate. A trip that normally takes two days. But, with a porter, who in addition to his headache had now also developed a sore leg, a guide whose chest infection wasn't going to improve at altitude and with Andre starting to lose his voice, and showing the same symptoms as Gideon had, we decided it's all the way off the mountain. At 2 minutes past 10 we stood at Stella Point. Apparently the descent from here to Barrafu camp takes about two to three hours. We did it in 59 minutes. Twenty minutes later, we left Barrafu and made our way to 'Mirrennium' (Millennium) camp where the crew were preparing lunch. While eating i said to Andre I'd love to get rid of my thermal bottom layer. But it would mean having to remove boots, trousers, socks. And with that came the realisation that every stitch of clothing I'm wearing has been on my body for about 36 hours... in the end i left the thermals on and didn't take anything off until i was safely in my hotel room where i could safely remove all the layers and dump them in a bag to be taken directly to a washing machine!

While the porters and our guides were having lunch Andre and I managed a quick but very welcome nap. And all too soon a much improved Gideon was calling us for the next leg of our descent - a muscle jarring final sixteen kilometres and more than 2000 vertical metres. A little over two and a half hours later we arrived at Mweka Gate, to hugs and cheers from our porters and porters from other parties we had passed on our way down. The only thing left to do for us, to sign out, pack the van, and drive to the nearest place that served cold beers, where we could treat ourselves and our porters to a cold drink and present them with a tip to say thanks for making it possible for us to have reached the top of Africa!

**Adrian Jardin**: Awesome. Well done. As Roland asked, are you going back to Mt Kenya ?

**Celeste Loots**: The conditions sound extreme! Don't think I could do that:( It sounds like your route was more difficult than the usual "tourist/fundraiser" route, yes? Take my hat off to you guys 😅🎩⛰

**HARRY**: Celeste: we summited during daylight hours. A definite advantage of the Western Breach Route... you don't have to get up at midnight to start walking in a human train with headlights up a scree slope... we did see the full moon the night before our ascent, rising above Uhuru, and the next night while in the crater. But due to the extreme cold and wind didn't have much time to enjoy it :)

**Barbara Wirz**: am in awe reading your gripping, jaw-dropping story...

**Paul Westcott**: Amazing story Harry! Well done for keeping us all on the edge of our seats with your adventure and experience and congratulations!

**HARRY**: There are probably pros and cons about each of the routes. On most other routes you are surrounded by (we estimated) as many as 500 people... we were on our own for three night. Starting early (5.30/6.00, you eliminate most of the risk associated with the Western Breach route.

**HARRY**: Roland, Adrian: see next and final instalment...

**HARRY**: What next? The quest having been to complete all three of Africa's highest peaks, means this challenge is far from over. I had the time and opportunity to return to Kenya and complete the climb, but since this challenge was started with Andre I intend finishing it with Andre. As soon as we possibly can return to the mountain, we will.

So far this has been a magnificent adventure! For me it started earlier this year when I went to Tenerife to climb Mt Teide. The one that Spanish bureaucracy denied me and will have to wait until later. From there I went to the Atlas Mountains in Morocco and despite a freezing wind that drove a lot of people of the mountain,  Hassan and I summited. Ethiopia was my next stop. Ras Dejen, the highest peak in the Simien Mountains turned out to be a completely different experience than to what I had expected. From there I joined with Andre, and for part of the way with Mandy, to climb Mt Stanley, Mt Kenya and Kilimanjaro.

Besides experiencing the diversity of the various mountains - from the snow covered Atlas overlooking the scorched earth of the Sahara, to the bird-rich and dramatic Simien mountains, the lush and green Ruwenzoris, Mt Kenya where only a glimpse of the peak was seen thanks to unseasonal bad weather, and finally on to Mt Kilimanjaro - the doyen of African mountains with its terrain ranging from enchanting rainforest to the desert-like crater below its summit, there was the equally diverse human experience. Hassan in Morocco, a Berber, who invited me to his house for dinner and whose text messages i have to decipher phonetically (e.g.: 'Hallo mfrin ioki' - which means "hallo my friend, are you okay?"). Amare, steady, reliable, a future associate. Based in Debarq, his experience ranging far beyond his native Simien mountains. Hoseinni, the 70+ year old scout who was my shadow in the Simiens, and who greeted me like a brother when i said goodbye. Yrga the cook, who was ex military and had seen service in the Sudan as well as Eritrea. A gentle soul who prepared great dishes for me and the team. Josephat and Bosco who guided us to the top of Mt Stanley. Technically the most difficult peak we ascended, involving ice climbing and a glacier crossing. At altitude! Moses. My partner and guide on previous excursions on Mt Kenya. And finally Gideon and Willy who guided us to the top of kilimanjaro, where our greatest challenge was the altitude. All people of Africa. All different. And yet, all the same. From 'darkest Africa' they may well be, but the blood that flows through their veins is a pure warm African red.

**Bridgette Blackmore**: Amazing! and your writing is just like reading a book but all the more intense that we're reading it so soon after the events :-). The porters and guides sound incredible!! Thank you for sharing your adventure Harry - B😊

**Celeste Loots**: I think I'd also prefer not to walk in the dark from midnight with crowds of others. Lovely to hear and see all without too much human interference:) I am reading about the stars and how they continually sing, if you listen closely you can hear them.

**Harry**: The stars, the wind, birds, water rushing past, the sound of the porters and guides chattering, your own footsteps... all part of the music

**Celeste Loots**: Sounds so rich with all the wonderful people you have made connections with. But that's part of your great art of friendship, that I've witnessed over the years:)

I hope Ryan is downloading all these writings and photos to put them together for you as the bones of your intended book! 🎩

**Paul Westcott**: Agree with Celeste Loots. You need to do a mini book 😊

**Pepi Malamoglou**: A book is a book Paul. Nothing mini about this one 📖📖😊

**Harry**: If I use large type, I will have enough pages for a book :)

**Pepi Malamoglou**: 😄😄😄 then we old topples won't need glasses to read it

**Pepi Malamoglou**: Toppies

**Harry**: Exactly :)

*Inside the Ash Pit...*

*Final glimpse of the Ash Pit*

*Making our way to Stella Point*

*Last view of the mountain on our descent...*

**Celeste Loots**: Amazing to see the Ash Pit! Nothing wrong with a short book with large print. Add lots of large size photos and it will be bigger 😄

**Rob Campbell**: Thank you Harry again for sharing your amazing adventure with us. You've given us a holiday. You've given us excitement. You've filled us with awe.

**Jean Landman**: Agree with Rob

**Charles Barry**:

**Bridgette Blackmore**: Blimey, that rock barrier looked scary!! I was trying to imagine it before the photo but the picture makes is look super scary!!

**Celeste Loots**: I think we should start up a just giving site for Harry's charity / fund straight away, for all of us who have had this fantastic opportunity to be in on this epic Challenge, to make a start to contributing. Aye?

**Megan MacFarlane**: Aye

**Roland Suhr**: Remind le Frog that absinthe makes the heart grow fonder. For the rest I join the chorus of thanks for well-composed pictures & interesting commentary.

**Paul Westcott**: Aye

---

## 24 August 2016

---

**Thea Groenewegen**: Well done Harry and Frog! You can put another feather in your cap! 💯!!✒️

**Theresa Rautenbach**:

**Lee Bennett**: Incredible. Thanks for including me in the group Harry. Am now keen to hear what's next!

**HARRY:** I was racking my brain yesterday to think if there was one particular event or moment during this adventure that stood out way above everything else.... Was there one memorable moment that defined this trip? For example, was getting to the top of Mt Stanley, technically the much more difficult and enjoyable peak, more satisfying than reaching the much higher Mt Kilimanjaro, the top of Africa? Was the trip in the Ruwenzoris with its lush and green more interesting than Mt Kenya where elephant and buffalo roam freely? I finally came to the conclusion that it was the people who were part of this trip that made it the most memorable! And that's not just the guides who lead us safely, or the porters who happily bounced along with loads of 20 or more kg on or suspended from their heads, nor the chefs that kept our stomachs happy, the hosts at the various places we stayed along the way, or my climbing partners on Mt Stanley, Mt Kenya and Kilimanjaro. It was also you! the people that were supporting me and us with your love, concern, care, encouragement: friends - some of whom I've known since pre-school days; the cousins that I've known forever; my children - one of whom constantly worried that i might be abducted by a stray terrorist somewhere; climbing and trekking partners on many adventures - details of some of which will only ever be known by a few (what happens in... stays in...); an ex-wife who has continued to support me in my love of adventure; the girlfriend who was lighting a candle on our behalf, on the very day that we were flying down the slopes of kilimanjaro; those who sent private messages of encouragement, support and love! You! You were the people that made this trip memorable! Thank you!!!!

**Pepi Malamoglou:** And that dear Harry is the very purpose of our limited time on this planet - to build relationships, love and be loved and in all you do be MAD (Make a difference) because that's what leaves the legacy. Bless you dear friend 💙💙

**Celeste Loots:** 💙💚💙 agree with Pepi- be blessed:)

**Thea Groenewegen:** So true! Your travelling partners can make or break a trip. Thanks for your kind words. Can't wait to see all your photo's! Since you are in Africa, why not commingeto SA as well?

**Paul Westcott:** Well said Pepi!

**Bridgette Blackmore:** A truly lovely sentiment Harry :-)

---

### 27 August 2016

---

**Peter Winder:** Hi Harry

It's been a real pleasure and thrill to follow your wonderful adventure and achievement. I've only commented once before (you know me) but I want you to know how proud I am to know the guy who completed this fantastic journey with your fantastic network of friends and supporters.

I look forward to welcoming you home.

Pete.

**Jèan-Prieur du Plessis**:

**Vince Nixon**: Ha Harry.

Would that I be younger and could join you on the top of the world. All three of them. Is Ryan in Italy now?

**Theresa Rautenbach**: I could not agree more with Peter. Am so proud to know you . You are truly living your life.

* * * * *

Harry Loots

# THANK YOU

To each and every one who supported us along the way. Both physically and mentally.

To the four people who spent many hours of their free time proof reading my book, suggested rewrites, corrected grammar, and spelling mistakes:

**Pete Swanepoel** who read and re-read almost all of the revisions and added corrections, context, advice. Pete and I had our first misadventures together when we were on a school tour to Namibia (formerly South West Africa) - he tells all in his blogpost: https://vrystaatconfessions.com/2015/09/01/south-west-africa/.

**John McMahon** who made me aware of my excessive use of exclamation marks and got rid of most of them and who is the undisputed leader of the Fairy Cave Gang.

**Adrian Jardin**, a climbing mate since the 1980s, more recently in the Dolomites, who picked up many more errors and suggested I tell people who Lucy and Yah are instead of assuming they know

And finally **André Dalais**, who has been a climbing mate since the late 1970s, and who has kept me entertained on many trips in the Drakensberg and other parts of South Africa, the Dolomites and on our epic adventure on Africa's three highest mountains. André did a sanity check and suggested a few more changes.

To the people who helped me select a cover: Adrian Jardin, André Dalais, Anita Henning, Ann Lake, Barbara Wirz, Jacquie du Toit, John McMahon, Pete Swanepoel, Thea Groenewegen, Theresa Rautenbach. Ann and Anita also suggested changes which I incorporated.

Thank you!

# BIBLIOGRAPHY

A list of the publications and resources I read and consulted:

Iain Allan, *Guide to Mount Kenya and Kilimanjaro* (African Books Collective; 5th revised edition, 1991)

Cameron M Burns, *Kilimanjaro and Mount Kenya: A Climbing and Trekking Guide* (Mountaineers Books, 1998)

Wielochowski, Andrew, *Kilimanjaro Map and Guide*, 1:75000 (EWP)

Wielochowski, Andrew, *Mount Kenya Map and Guide*, 1:50,000 (EWP, 2007)

Paddy Dillon, *Walking on Tenerife: 45 walks including El Teide and GR131* (Cicerone Guide, 2015)

Ernest Hemingway, *The Snows of Kilimanjaro* (First published in Esquire magazine, 1936). The version I read was an eBook published by Simon & Schuster UK Ltd in 2014

Meyer, Hans (Dr), *Across East African Glaciers: An Account of the First Ascent of Kilimanjaro* (First published in 1891). The version I read was an eBook downloaded without publisher information.

Eva Melusine Thieme, *Kilimanjaro Diaries: Or, How I Spent a Week Dreaming of Toilets, Drinking Crappy Water, and Making Bad Jokes While Having the Time of My Life*, (Kindle Edition, 2014)

Wikipedia was a useful source of information, as were various other websites where I picked up odd bits of information, which helped in the planning of routes, and logistics of getting to, across, and from the mountains.

Harry Loots

I've tried to name the people that I've had adventures with somewhere in the world's wild places. Or met along the way while in these wild places. Be they in the mountains in South Africa, the UK, Europe, elsewhere on the African continent, Middle East, Asia. There's every possibility that I have forgotten some names here… If I have please remind me.

Freddy Gray (RIP), Gerard Hansen (RIP), JP De Witt, Andre Landman, Pierre du Plessis, Peter (Koos) Swanepoel, Tuffy Joubert, Greg Aligianis, Pierre Viljoen, Sheila Swanepoel, Derrick Mileham, Rudolph (Gabba) Coetzee (RIP), Ferdi van Rooyen, Mark van Staden, Dave Monk, Vince Nixon, Charles Barry, Kobus Gerber, Danie Geyer, Roland Wilkinson, Brian Shuttleworth (RIP), Colin Shuttleworth (RIP), Hannes Boshoff, Marina Boshoff, Rodney Owen (RIP), Des Watkins (RIP), Vic van Reenen (RIP), Vera Acton, André Dalais, Adrian Jardin, Adrian Hill, Roy Gooden, Steve Salmon, Clem Robbins, Maggie Salmon, Fred Rodwell (RIP), Chris Rodwell, Roland Suhr, Dave Easton, Alf Cass, Chris Handley, Geoff Ingham, Rolf Person, Charles Meth, Hannie Low, Mervyn Gans, Allison Gans, Carl Fatti (RIP), Anna Fatti, Paul Fatti, Jaap Earle, Eckhardt Haber, Elise Haber, Clive Ward, Fiona Jones, Evan Jones, Ulrike Kiefer, Sharn Brummer, Charl Brummer, Cuan Cronje, Rudie Clayton, Ed Salomons, Lesley Foehr, Steven Bradshaw, Rob Guest, Jan Guest, Herman Behrens, Paul Behrens, Dougal Drummond (RIP), Lynn Drummond, Angus Drummond, Ian Drummond, Rowan Drummond, Doug Lyon, Rose Lyon, Wiv von Willich (RIP), Joan von Willich (RIP), Ilse von Willich, Chris Steenkamp (RIP), Lorraine Steenkamp (RIP), Frank du Toit, Herman Kuhne, Tjaart van der Walt, Giel Prins, Christine Glasspool, Rob Campbell, Beryl Gronland, Colin Gibson, Henriette Gibson, Julie-Anne Moors, William Gibson, Jane Hill, Jan van der Velden, Frikkie van Zyl, Zelda Willemse, Richard Groenewegen, Thea Groenewegen, Gary Gifford, Gill Tresise, Gerhard Lamprecht, the 1st Newcastle

Scouts that kept me on my toes: Bruce and Greg Perry, Rick and Lester Welgemoed, Kevan (RIP) and Sean McQuade, Ted and the Goebel boys Don and Gary, Ivan and Denis Venter, Thomas Leach, Des Horner, Justin Ryan, Chris Walsham, Ewald Viljoen, Kevin Oliver, Andrew Edwards, Stoffel de Jager, Craig Hilton-Taylor, Keith Cooper (RIP), Steve Piper, Mike Scott, Derek Paul, Micky Williams, Linda Antoncich, Martin Yodaiken, Ed February, Chris Lomax, Jono Fisher, Guy Holwill, Andi Tromp, Deon Tromp, Adelle McCann, Tinie Versfeld, Michael Schaff, Paul Schlotfeldt, Tim Wilmot, Garth Hattingh (RIP), Judy Moore, Brent Jennings, Ross Suter, Alf Bam, Jeremy Samson, Duncan Nderitu, Moses Njagi (RIP), Simon Maina, Ronaldo Mvungi, Mohamed Khader, Andy Borthwick, Theresa Aram, John McMahon, Simon Harris, Sandy Creighton, Frank Kosterman, Anke Hafmans, Antonella Trabiuo, Jacquie du Toit, Louis Wessels, Steven Haxell, James Howlett, Leslie Kett, Courtney Blodgett, Karolin Wladar, Julia Schwarz, Alessandro Fiori, Berthold Kaib, Amare Melkam, Majka Maroza, Manuela Miglioranzi, Marko Glätzer, Mike McGrath, Kaat Van de Paer, Kristijn van Riel, Loke Pollier, Gaby Anvidalfarei, Dagmar Frontull, and many more… and Barbara who puts up with me not only on the mountains but during the week as well.

# ABOUT THE AUTHOR

Harry Loots was born in Harrismith in South Africa, where he took his first steps up a mountain. He has lived and worked and climbed in South Africa, UK, Netherlands, Germany, Italy, Hong Kong, and Switzerland.

He currently lives in Zürich in Switzerland with his girlfriend, Barbara. They spend most weekends in various parts of the Alps, and holidays on mountains further away. Harry shares their experiences in his blog, https://mountain-paths.com/.

His three children are all grown up and have children of their own. Some of whom may become climbers like their Grandad…

Harry recently started a new company organising trips to African mountains. He has a simple philosophy for having started the company: to connect people who love the mountains with Africa's greatest mountains; and to make sure that the guides, cooks, and porters who support them, get a wage worthy of their efforts. Sadly, many of the guides, cooks and porters are desperate for work, and will work for a quarter or less of what they should be paid. Often, they have to provide their own food and equipment while on the mountain, so that the less ethical tour operators can put extra money in their own pockets.

His company is called Walk in Wild Places (https://walkinwildplaces.com), and he would love to help you get to the top of Africa's mountains.